How to .
Living as a Writer

JAMES SCOTT BELL

Compendium Press

How to Make a Living as a Writer

ISBN: 978-0-910355-16-2

Compendium Press
P.O. Box 705
Woodland Hills, CA 91365

Cover design by Josh Kenfield

About the Author

James Scott Bell is the #1 bestselling author of *Plot & Structure, Write Your Novel From The Middle, The Art of War for Writers, Revision & Self-Editing for Publication* and several other books on the writing craft. His popular workshops have been taught all over the world. He is a bestselling and award-winning thriller author, and is the first self-published author to be nominated for an International Thriller Writers Award.

He lives and writes in his hometown, Los Angeles.

His website is www.jamesscottbell.com.

Also by James Scott Bell

Writing

Plot & Structure
Revision & Self-Editing for Publication
The Art of War for Writers
Conflict & Suspense
Write Your Novel From the Middle
How to Write Dazzling Dialogue
How to Make a Living as a Writer

Thrillers

Don't Leave Me
Blind Justice
Final Witness
Watch Your Back
One More Lie
Deceived
Try Dying
Try Darkness
Try Fear

The Trials of Kit Shannon series

City of Angels (with Tracie Peterson)
Angels Flight (with Tracie Peterson)
Angel of Mercy (with Tracie Peterson)
A Greater Glory
A Higher Justice
A Certain Truth

Contents

1. Why I Wrote This Book

Let's get one thing straight from the jump. I have this quaint notion that it's okay for writers to make money from their writing. Maybe even make a living.

Astounding, I know. But I believe it. And celebrate it.

Because for most of human history the vast majority of writers have been lucky to make lunch money from their scribblings. Very few have been able to support themselves from the quill or the keyboard alone.

But that's all changed.

I've been writing for my bread for almost twenty years now. Writing is the only profession I ever really wanted to pursue. I got sidetracked into law for a while. That's because I didn't think I had what it takes to be a writer.

In college I got to be in a workshop with Raymond Carver, and quickly realized I couldn't just sit down and write beautiful prose. I thought that's what you had to be able to do if you were a true writer.

The people around me kept saying writing was not something you could learn. You especially couldn't learn it from craft books, which were sniffed at by the cognoscenti as a waste of money.

I believed that flapdoodle for about ten years.

But the writing bug came back to me with a vengeance. I knew I had to try to learn to write fiction, even it was futile, because that's what I wanted to do with my life.

And lo and behold, I found out the naysayers were dead wrong.

You Can Learn What You Need to Know

On September 15, 1990, I wrote these words in my journal:

> EPIPHANY!
> Light! A bulb! A flash! A revelation! My muse on fire!
> I feel like I've suddenly "clicked into" how to write . . . I mean, everything I've been reading and brooding about has finally locked. There is this tremendous rush of exhilaration. It just happened, and now I feel like everything I write will be at least GOOD, but can also be EXCELLENT.

I was writing screenplays at the time and I'd written five or six over two years without much encouragement, let alone success. But the next one I wrote was optioned and got me into an agency. I optioned other scripts, too, and did some assignment work (including a treatment for the late, great Whitney Houston). But when the projects didn't get pushed up the ladder (an old Hollywood story) I got frustrated and wrote a novel using the same revealed wisdom. The novel sold. Then I wrote a legal thriller and got a five-book contract. My career as a novelist was launched.

And all of it I trace back to that epiphany.

Which carries an important lesson for those who desire to make a go of a writing career: you *can* learn what you need to know.

And you can know enough to have a real shot at making a living at this or, at least, create a healthy stream of income that can keep on flowing and growing.

More writers are making real dough than at any time in the history of the written word. The digital revolution—which began on November of 2007 with the introduction of the Kindle—has given innumerable writers a whole new way to grow abundant lettuce in their literary gardens.

What I want to give you in this book are the creative and business principles that have worked for me and other successful writers I've observed. But what I need to make clear now is that none of this is a get-rich-quick proposition. While there have been some fabulous monetary successes of late, in both traditional and self-publishing, it's never been easy to support oneself by writing alone.

In what's called the Pulp era, roughly 1920 - 1950, many writers put food on the table being prolific providers of stories. Most of them lived modestly in order to write full time. It was hard work, but they saw it as a job like any other.

When the "slick" magazines took off in the 1950s, a new breed of writer, the freelancer, sprang up. Working just as hard as their pulp cousins, they made their living by coming up with article ideas by the truckload, querying multiple magazines on a daily basis, and making relationships with editors as a means of securing future assignments.

Both the pulp and freelance writers would try to turn some of their material into books. When these got published, it was another source of income.

None of this was easy work. But it was writing, and that's what they wanted to do.

Every now and then one of these writers would have a breakout success that actually did lead to what many would call wealth. It's happening today, too, though it's rare. It may even happen for you, but don't go into this *expecting* that you'll go real estate shopping in The Hamptons. If it happens, great. Invite me to the housewarming.

But if you want to make a living — or at least a substantial part of a living — off of your writing, get ready to work for it. I want to help you work smart. I want to increase your chances of making good in this game.

Did I say *game?* Yes. You've got to look at it that way. It's part skill and part chance. If you up your skill and take more chances, your odds of success increase.

There's a lot of chatter these days about writing success being like a lottery. Something about that metaphor has always bothered me. For in a true lottery you can't affect your odds (except by buying more tickets, of course). But is that true for writers?

I don't think it is. Just putting more books out there ("buying more tickets") won't help your chances if the books don't generate reader interest and loyalty. Productivity is a virtue, but to that must be added *value*.

Hugh Howey, one of the most successful self-publishing writers out there, had some interesting thoughts on timing and luck on his blog of March 17th, 2014 (see HughHowey.com). Citing Malcolm Gladwell's book *Outliers*, Howey highlighted a fascinating factoid:

> A list of the 75 wealthiest people in history, which goes all the way back to Cleopatra, shows that 20% were Americans born within 9 years of each other. Between 1831 to 1840, a group that includes Rockefeller, Carnegie, Armour, J.P. Morgan, George Pullman, Marshall Field, and Jay Gould were born. They all became fabulously wealthy in the United States in the 1860s and 1870s, just as the railroad and Wall Street and other industries were exploding.

From this Howey explains how he benefitted from being in the right place at the right time, Kindle-wise. He had started writing in earnest in 2009, just as the neo-self-publishing movement was taking off. He did some things right, like early adoption of KDP Select and serialization. Look at him now.

But there is one thing he says I disagree with: "I know I'm not that good."

Wrong. He is good. Very good. *Wool* would not be what it is without the quality. Which Howey has worked hard to achieve.

Reminds me of the old adage, "Luck is where hard work meets opportunity." I believe that wholeheartedly.

Skill Increases Your Odds

So I wouldn't call the publishing biz a lottery system. What metaphor would I use? It hit me one day: writing success is more like my favorite game, backgammon.

Backgammon, which has been around for 5,000 years, is brilliantly conceived. Dice are involved, so there's always an element of chance. Someone who is way behind still might win if the dice give him a roll he needs at a crucial moment.

On the other hand, someone who knows how to think strategically, can calculate odds, and takes risks at the right time will win more often than the average player who depends mostly on the rolling bones.

Early on I studied the game by reading books. I memorized the best opening moves for each roll. I learned how to think about what's called the "back game," what the best "points" are to cover, and when it might pay off to leave a "blot."

And I played a lot of games with friends and, later, on a computer. I discovered a couple of killer, though risky, opening moves. I use them because they can pay off big time, though when they don't I find myself behind. But I'm willing to take these early chances because they are not foolhardy and I'm confident enough in my skills that I can still come back.

This, it seems to me, is more analogous to the writing life than a lottery. Yes, there is chance involved. I sold my first novel because I happened to be at a convention with an author I had met on the plane. This new acquaintance showed me around the floor, introduced me to people. One of them was a publisher he knew. That publisher just happened to be starting a new publishing house and was looking for material. I pitched him my book and he bought it a few weeks later.

Chance.

But I was also ready for that moment. I had been studying the craft for several years and was committed to a weekly quota of words. I'd written several screenplays and at least one messy novel before completing the project I had with me at the convention.

Work.

Thus, as in backgammon, the greater your skill, the better your chances. The harder you work, the more skill you acquire. Sure, there are different talent levels, but that's not something we have any control over.

Biology, however, is not destiny. Someone with less talent who works hard often outperforms the gifted.

Now, that doesn't mean you'll always win big in any one game. Far from it. If the dice are not your friends, things might not turn out as planned. That book you thought was a sure winner might sink.

But don't stop playing.

And don't ever worry about the dice. You cannot control them, not even if you shake them hard and shout, "Baby needs a new pair of shoes!" The vagaries of the book market are out of your hands. You can, however, control your work ethic and awareness of opportunity.

Note this, too. Even if your writing efforts do not show quite the returns you aimed for at first, you may still create an income stream that is steady and significant. You might then reach a point where you can move to a part-time "day job" that is to your liking while allowing you to devote more time to your writing.

There are so many options now.

Writing success is therefore not a lottery.

It's a game.

The trick is to play intelligently, play a lot and try to have some fun, too.

My hope is that this book will help you do all of that.

2. The 7 Secrets of Writing Success

Over the course of time I've observed many writers rise through the ranks and achieve professional status. Some have gone on to make substantial incomes and long-term careers. A number of them were students in my workshops, which gave me a good opportunity to analyze what characteristics they have in common.

I've spotted seven that dominate.

Seven that you can replicate in your own writing life.

1. Love

"You must want it *enough*. Enough to take all the rejections, enough to pay the price of disappointment and discouragement while you are learning. Like any other artist you must learn your craft—then you can add all the genius you like." – Phyllis Whitney

An inner fire to make it as a writer is what will get you through years of cold reality.

I'm of the opinion that you ought to have more than the mere desire to make money. The majority of writers who make it to full-time status love what they do. They have to, because the early returns are almost always skimpy.

Do you have that love? Is writing your calling?

When I was just starting out on my writing life I saw a photograph of Stephen King, early in his career, with his feet up on his desk and his dog underneath. He was dressed casually and going over a manuscript. I knew that was the kind of working life I wanted. I put that picture up in my office.:

I'd look at that picture each day and let the *feeling* sink in.

Then I would act on the feeling. I would write.

That's the important part.

When you feel the desire, turn it into energy at the keyboard.

Repeat this over and over, daily, weekly, yearly...and you will begin to get the feeling of being unstoppable.

I must mention here that there is also a toxic form of love and desire (the stuff of many classic novels, of course). That's when you want something so much you get embittered if you don't get it, or you begin to envy others who have what you don't.

It's a careful balancing act. I have more to say on that in the chapter titled Make a Life, Not Just a Living.

For now, let positive love fuel your fire.

2. Discipline

"Even if there is a price to be paid, don't be afraid to use appropriate discipline. It may hurt in the short term, but it will pay dividends in the future I believe one of the big lessons of sports for dedicated individuals and teams is that it shows us how hard work, and I mean hard work, does pay dividends. The great dividend is not necessarily outscoring an opponent. The guaranteed dividend is the complete peace of mind gained in knowing you did everything within your power, physically, mentally, and emotionally, to bring forth your full potential." – John Wooden, legendary UCLA basketball coach

As a high school basketball player, I got to go to the John Wooden basketball camp one summer. He was at the height of his fame then, the most successful college coach, in any sport, of all time.

What was his secret? It was his disciplined approach to hard work and fundamentals. You learned the fundamentals, and practiced them, over and over. This was, quite often, sheer drudgery. We all wanted to get out on the floor and play!

But the discipline paid off. When we did get out on the court we were much better players. That's why Wooden had so many of his boys make it to the pros. Even if they weren't stars, they could often have a long and respectable career.

Because of discipline.

Writers, you need it too, if you want to have a shot of making a living at your vocation.

3. Perseverance

"The brick walls are there for a reason. The brick walls are not there to keep us out. The brick walls are there to give us a chance to show how badly we want something. Because the brick walls are there to stop the people who don't want it badly enough. They're there to stop the other people." – Randy Pausch, *The Last Lecture*

If you love to write, it's always too soon to quit.

If things aren't working out as fast as you want them to, don't give up. Figure out what you can be doing differently, and then try that.

It may mean writing a different kind of book.

Or it may mean writing the same kind of book even better.

But the true writer puts this thought in mind: *I am going to write and never stop because that's what I want to do. I will keep learning and growing and producing the words. I'll keep carving out time to write, even if it means giving some things up. Because this is what I want to do. This is why it's always too soon to quit.*

4. A Sound Mind

By which I mean the ability to overcome emotionalism and see things objectively. To take some of the hard knocks that are part of the writer's life and turn them into opportunities to grow stronger.

One of the key mental disciplines to develop is the ability to *slay expectations.*

It's okay to desire things and it is good to set goals and try to attain them. But expectations are killers.

An expectation is an obligation you place on the future. But the future has its own ideas and it's all out of your control. If the future doesn't meet your expectations, you suffer. You are disappointed, even to the point of despair.

Try with all your might not to set up expectations. Concentrate on your pages, your craft, and do your best. Then let your books out into the world to do what they do.

The ancient Stoics got this one right. Epictetus said, "There is only one way to happiness and that is to cease worrying about things which are beyond the power of our will."

That's having a sound mind.

5. Business Savvy

"Drive thy business or it will drive thee." – Benjamin Franklin

If you want to make a living as a writer, you have to approach writing and publishing as a business.

A successful business makes a profit. To make a profit you need a plan.

Many writers and other artists shudder at this notion. Some even rebel against it. For them writing success is usually an accident.

I don't want you to be an accident. I want you to think like an entrepreneur. Even if you work with an agent and/or publisher, do not leave all business decisions to others. You simply can't afford to do that anymore. The successful writer is the informed writer.

"Our general conclusion is that self-publishing is beginning to mature. While it continues to be a force to reckon with, it is evolving from a frantic, wild-west style space to a more serious business," said Beat Barblan, Bowker Director of Identifier Services, in 2014. "The market is stabilizing as the trend of self-publisher as business-owner, rather than writer only, continues."

The good news is that basic business principles are not hard to understand. It's just a matter of putting them into practice.

I cover those principles in the next chapter.

6. A Support System

Writing is, by and large, a lonely life. As author Peter Straub once put it: "Every writer must acknowledge and be able to handle the unalterable fact that he has, in effect, given himself a life sentence in solitary confinement."

Thus, what every writer needs is support from other people.

Being with a writer can be tough, because our minds wander. We watch interesting people at a restaurant. We eavesdrop. Our brains tune out a conversation as we suddenly start thinking about our WIP.

Whenever I go to a hospital to visit someone, I must confess that half my mind is thinking, *Hm, this would make a good detail in a scene....*

So give a little grace to your loved ones and friends. Take time to hang out with positive people and winnow out those who drag you down.

Seek the fellowship of other writers. A writers conference is a great way to meet other scribes. Email makes it easy to keep in touch. Consider forming a circle of such friends.

Use the law of reciprocity. You tend to get back what you give. Be a support to others and you will be supported in return.

It's always good to know that while you may write alone, you're not alone in life.

7. Talent

"Unrewarded genius is almost a proverb." – Calvin Coolidge

This is by far the least important item.

That's right, the least.

First of all, there's no real measurement for talent. It's a subjective thing. There is no final arbiter of what constitutes talent. It's a little like what a Supreme Court justice once said about obscenity: I can't define it, but I know it when I see it.

You do have to have some ability to string sentences together in a coherent fashion. This is a matter of education and the habit of reading.

Winston Churchill, one of the great men of the twentieth century, is mainly known today as the Prime Minister of England during that country's darkest hour, World War II. His steel character and stirring speeches helped inspire his nation and keep the Nazis at bay. What is not so much remembered is that he won the Nobel Prize for Literature!

To what did he attribute his ability to write the kind of prose that would win the ultimate prize? His reading at a young age, when he was getting the sound"of the English sentence firmly planted in his brain.

At the end of this book I have a suggested reading list, both fiction and non-fiction. Some of the books are challenging, but you need a challenge to grow your ability to write.

One thing I suggest: both read and listen to books. Listening to audio books puts the rhythm of the language in your brain by a different route. The more routes, the better.

Further: do what many writers of old used to do—copy passages of books word for word. Write them out in long hand.

Get words into your head!

Study vocabulary. Increase the number of words you know. Even though our culture is headed downhill as far as reading comprehension, the more you know the language, the better off you'll be.

3. The 8 Essentials of Your Writing Business

As stated in the previous chapter, if you want to make a living as a writer, you are not just a writer.

You are a business.

Wrap your head around that now and it will save you a lot of trouble in the future.

Business principles are simple to understand. The real challenge is implementation.

The great thing about your publishing business is that the startup costs are microscopic compared to other businesses. You don't have to pay for office space or warehousing. You don't have to buy inventory or pay a staff.

You do have to pay for quality prep. But other than that your only real investment is time.

Another advantage is that you do not have to fear the growth of your business. In other lines too much growth too fast can actually be a disaster. Not so with the writing business. As you grow you make more dough. That's about it.

1. Know What Your Customers Want and How to Deliver it to Them

People who read want one of two things: knowledge or entertainment. When you can give them both, so much the better.

For example, if you're a novelist, your first job is to entertain. No, it's not to deliver a message. As movie mogul Samuel Goldwyn once put it, "If you want to send a message try Western Union."

Sure, you can write to uphold a theme or argue a point. Ayn Rand saw herself primarily as a philosopher. But she was trained as a screenwriter. She knew she wouldn't be heard if she didn't write first to entertain.

Learn to tell a story readers won't want to put down. Everything else is secondary for the novelist, because if a reader doesn't read your book it doesn't matter what your message is.

Now, if you can add knowledge to your entertainment—say, a picture of how a real FBI agent operates under unique circumstances—you are cooking with both gas jets. Readers of fiction love to pick up inside knowledge like that.

For the writer of non-fiction, knowledge is the main thrust of the book. Readers want to find out how to do something, be something, get more happiness, get more money, find out about a person or place or period of history, and so on.

If you can give that to them *and* be entertaining, so much the better. If your voice and style are a pleasure to read as you provide the essential information, you are delivering ultimate value.

The three-volume biography of Winston Churchill by William Manchester is an example. The first two pages are the best opening of any book of any kind I've ever read. All the rest is a pleasure to read.

Make it your goal to deliver entertainment and knowledge in both your fiction and non-fiction.

Did I just say both?

Yes, because you should...

2. Think Multiple Streams of Writing Income

In the "old days" of professional writing (i.e., before 2007 and the introduction of the Kindle), most freelance writers made their living by writing for multiple markets. They would study what magazines wanted and then propose articles based on those needs. If they delivered quality it was likely the editor of the magazine would offer them more work.

They learned to become experts in several markets so if one stream dried up there would be others to go back to.

They would then write books on the subjects they became expert in.

Some of them dabbled in fiction. Short stories, novels, genre pieces for publications like *Analog* and *Alfred Hitchcock's Mystery Magazine*.

In this new world of digital self-publishing, it's easier than ever to test waters and try new things. Your only limitation is your own production schedule.

If you are a fiction writer, don't limit yourself just to fiction (unless you want to). When my fiction career started to take off, it was after years of diligently studying the craft. I began teaching workshops on what I'd learned. It then occurred to me that I could start a non-fiction stream as an expert on the writing craft. I proposed a book to Writer's Digest Books called *Plot & Structure*. It was a natural fit for me.

When the book took off I proposed another to WD, and it was accepted. I've done four books in all for WD and the royalties from those books make up one of my streams.

I've self-published writing books like this one. That's a stream, too. Another is writing specialized material for the legal profession.

I consider myself a fiction writer first. It's what I love most. But I also enjoy writing non-fiction. I'm continuing to explore other subjects of interest to write about, even as I keep fiction on the front burner.

Is there a non-fiction subject that fits you? Perhaps it comes out of the research for your novel. What if you write a police procedural and become conversant with your local police department's manner of doing things. This could become a short book for writers on how to write police procedurals. Or maybe there's a particular case a detective tells you about. This might become fodder for a non-fiction, true crime book.

But don't feel like you have to stay within the parameters of your novels. If you want to write about a subject you like, there's nothing stopping you. For more on this, see the chapter How to Write Non-Fiction for Profit.

Each of the following is another opportunity to write for pay. You can explore the possibilities via

Google or books on the various subjects, which include:

- Copywriting
- Ghostwriting
- Writing for corporate e-zines
- Speech writing
- Writing business reports
- Technical journal writing

You may also wish to check out a site called Textbroker.com. Through this service you set up an author account and go through an acceptance process. Once that's done you use the service to browse writing jobs listed by Textbroker clients. These are usually businesses seeking some form of content (e.g., blog posts, product descriptions). You connect, write, and get paid according to a scale. It's not going to make you rich, but it can be another of your streams. See the site for details.

Here is the good news if you know how to write readable prose: most people don't, and that includes people in big businesses. If you can string sentences together logically and clearly, you will have no problem finding places that need your abilities. And while this kind of writing is not going to make you wealthy, it is guaranteed writing income that can be steady and welcome.

How does this fit with the "write what you love" ideal? The key is to respect the words you write enough to be proud of what you produce. For example, I love shaping my weekly blog posts for the Kill Zone. It makes me happy to use the principles of good, literate non-fiction. Just as a brick mason can take pleasure in building someone a wall with the tools of his craft, so too can a writer find satisfaction in an article written on assignment.

I also want to mention the Kindle Singles program. In 2011, Amazon opened up a platform primarily for writing that is shorter than a traditional book. Several authors have made five- and even six-figure income through this program.

Amazon explains it this way:

> We're looking for compelling ideas expressed at their natural length--writing that doesn't easily fall into the conventional space limitations of magazines or print books. Kindle Singles are typically between 5,000 and 30,000 words.

A Kindle Single can be on any topic — fiction, essays, memoirs, reporting, personal narratives, profiles, and so on.

To nominate your self-published book you email kindle-singles@amazon.com and include the title, ASIN (Amazon's digital identifier which they have assigned to your work) and a brief summary of your piece.

If your work is not yet published, you can submit a manuscript or a pitch. Note that all manuscripts submitted as attachments must be accompanied by a cover letter with a detailed summary of the submission.

3. Create a Business Plan

Every business success is based on a plan of action. A plan gives you direction and a roadmap that will keep you going when things get confusing.

A business plan can always be modified, but without a plan you're a bottle in the ocean—you don't know what shore you're going to wash up on.

Start your planning by figuring out:

Where does your most enjoyable writing meet actual commercial possibility?

Writing what you are passionate about is a good thing. But if you want to make a living at it you have to sell enough to bring in a profit.

And that means objectively analyzing the marketplace.

For example, based on several sources, the most popular genres of fiction usually shake down to:

1. Romance
2. Mysteries
3. Historical
4. Thrillers
5. Paranormal
6. Science Fiction/Fantasy
7. Contemporary Women's Fiction
8. Young Adult
9. Horror
10. Crime

Do you write in one of the genres? If not, can you?

Yes, you can.

I believe a writer should love his genres. But you can *learn* to love a genre. Sort of like an arranged marriage.

Nicholas Sparks did this with his own career. He went into it like a businessman. He looked at the bestselling genres and discovered that each one had two big names that dominated. At the same time, a surprise book emerged called *The Bridges of Madison County.* It was a tear-jerking love story written by a male author. And it exploded.

Sparks decided he could be the second name on this unique subset — men who write tear-jerking love stories.

He's done pretty well.

But what about *literary* fiction, the kind of enduring novels that are studied in college classrooms? What if you want to write something like *To Kill a Mockingbird* or *The Catcher in the Rye?*

Reality check. Most agents and editors, if they are speaking off the cuff, will admit that literary writing is defined as the kind that does not sell. The finalists for the National Book Award each year routinely sell between 2000 – 5000 copies, and that's it.

As respected crime writer David Corbett once put it, this is the sort of literature that can turn a writer into "one of the highly respected and widely unread."

It has always been so. Evan Hunter *(The Blackboard Jungle)* wanted to be a huge success as a literary novelist. But he had to support his family, so he adopted the pen name Ed McBain and wrote police procedurals on the side.

Ed McBain became wealthy and world famous. Evan Hunter never quite forgave him for that.

If literary writing is tough sell in the traditional world, it's even tougher for the self-publisher. Writing fiction for a living is all about what the pulp writer Jack Woodford called "cash-and-carry prose."

It has been posited that the self-publishing revolution and the need for commercial success are choking off the curation of literary fiction. Sadly, this is true. I say sadly because I love literary fiction. I've been moved and even shaped by great lit-fic from past and present. I hope such books will continue to be published.

But the writer who wants to make serious money has to look at the world as it is and not just as he hopes it will be. Writing for income means taking stock of real marketplace possibilities and then putting your own unique voice into the material. Which means you should...

4. Define Your Unique Selling Proposition (USP)

A new business has to know what it is offering customers that they can't get anywhere else. The selling proposition needs to be unique in order to differentiate it in the marketplace.

As a writer, can you define what it is that readers will get from you that only you can give them?

And don't say, "My voice." Or "My expertise."

Define it as specifically as you can. Be bold about it. Talk yourself up.

Example: "I write romances that are about quirky characters no reader can possibly resist. I bring to these books a view about what makes lovers tick that is warm and wise and even educational about why two people become soul mates. I base this on my God-given insight into human nature and my own experiences in love—the good, the bad and the ugly!"

Example: "I write books on how to take care of yourself in a world of increasingly nasty people. And I do it in a way that's easy to understand and put into action. I write in a voice that is blunt, sometimes funny, but always full of the practical and life-affirming advice. I am the new Chuck Norris (but please don't tell Chuck I said that)."

Okay, now it's your turn. Write up a USP for every genre of writing you are pursuing. Play with these. Show them to others. Tweak them until they start to excite you.

The publishing word for this is *branding*. In the days of print-only, branding was largely determined by physical shelf space and seasonal purchases by bookstores. An author could not come out with several different titles at roughly the same time. Bookstores wouldn't buy. They also wouldn't know where to shelve an author's books if they were of different genres.

Almost always a genre writer, once consigned to a shelf "ghetto," could not get out. That's why many authors chose pseudonyms to write in other genres.

There are no such limitations in the digital world. All books are "shelved" cover out. Digitized books are given, via algorithm, space next to similar books. A reader can find new authors in a genre this way.

The use of a pseudonym is no longer necessary. In fact, some readers of one of your brands may cross over to the other ones.

However, be sure to distinguish your brands via the cover art and book descriptions.

5. Know How to Handle Finances

As a small business, with ebbs and flows in how you are paid, you have to know how to manage your money. There are short-term and long-term aspects to this.

Short-term, know what fees are reasonable for the services you need (e.g., cover design and editing). Carefully review all such transactions to measure the ROI (return on investment). Make adjustments as needed. Look for new possibilities and test them. For example, if you find a freelance editor who looks promising, ask for a two-page sample edit before paying for the full service.

Long-term: I've always tried lived by the immortal advice of Wilkins Macawber in *David Copperfield*: "Annual income twenty pounds, annual expenditure nineteen nineteen and six, result happiness. Annual income twenty pounds, annual expenditure twenty pounds ought and six, result misery."

By the way, if you want to make a living as a writer, where you live makes a difference. I live in Los Angeles. It's where I grew up and I love it. It's expensive here. So my level of income has to be of a certain magnitude. I produce what I do in order to continue living in my home town.

But you don't have to live in a place so expensive. You can write anywhere. Your writing production and income will be the same whether you live in New

York or Oklahoma City. It's your cost of living that will be different.

6. Be Action Oriented

All the planning in the world means squat unless it is acted upon. You must take some action every day in order to succeed.

As a writer, the most important action is: producing the words.

That means you write to a quota.

Start now by looking at your weekly schedule and finding all the time you can dedicate to writing. Make it your aim to find time to write every day, six days a week. (I advocate taking one day a week off from writing. This "writing Sabbath" enables your brain to recharge. I find I'm more creative and energized if I allow myself that one day off).

Of course, not everyone can find daily writing time. The demands of a full-time job or duties at home make wrting time limited. If you can't write every day, pick your spots and make appointments with yourself to fill them.

Do what you can and don't worry about it. The key is consistency. Simply figure out how many words you can *comfortably* produce per week.

Once you've done that, raise that total word count by 10%. You need a little bit of stretch beyond your comfort zone.

This weekly total is your quota. As you find more time to write, you can increase it.

Divide that total by six (remember, you're taking a day off). That's the daily average to shoot for, but it's flexible and accounts for life's interruptions. If you miss a day of writing, you can make up your word count on the other days.

For example, if I'm writing 1,000 words a day, six days a week, and I miss a day, I can look at my remaining days and re-calibrate. If I have three writing days left in my week, I'll aim for 1,333 words each day.

That 1,000 would be my minimum, by the way. If I'm cooking I will blast on past that count. If I happen to do 2,500 words in a day, I will still aim for 1,000 the other days. But if one of those days comes up where I can't write, I've got a built-in pad.

Keep track of your daily writing on a spreadsheet. Record the number of words you write each day, project by project. Words that you add when editing count.

You don't have to subtract words you cut.

Have your spreadsheet add up your weekly word count. At the end of the year, add up all the words.

This practice will get you in the habit of doing the single most important thing you can do as a writer: write words.

Other actions to take once a day:

- Spend some time editing projects.
- Spend time overseeing your published projects.
- Set a time for social media, and stick to that time. Don't get lost in the vortex.

Actions you should take at least once a week:

- Spend one half hour in pure creativity time. (See the chapter on Unlocking Your Creative Genius)

- Spend one hour studying your craft—reading books, *Writer's Digest* magazine, trusted blogs.

Monthly:

- Spend time networking with other writers, via email or critique groups. Join an organization like Mystery Writers of America or Romance Writers of America, and go to local meetings.

Once a year:

- Take a business planning retreat. One day all to yourself thinking about and re-visioning your writing business.
- Go to a good writers conference. This is a valuable investment of your time and will pay dividends in increased knowledge and networking.

7. Be About Quality Control and Constant Improvement

A successful business stays successful by making sure everything in their process is quality and, when it isn't, figuring out how to improve it.

This is no less true for the successful writer.

Everything about your self-published book, for example, needs quality: editing, cover design, formatting, book description and, of course, the book itself.

You get quality by working with quality people. If you need to pay a little extra for a great editor, it's worth it. Ditto a cover designer.

Don't cut corners on quality.

Test the quality with others. Get opinions. For my fiction, I always go out to a group of beta readers before doing anything else.

I run cover designs by my wife and kids.

There is nothing I do that is solely on my own. If I believe strongly in something, I advocate for it. But if I get a strong argument in return, I am willing to relent.

In addition to quality, I want to periodically analyze what I'm doing to see how I might improve.

I never stop studying the craft of writing.

I never stop learning about the business of both traditional and self-publishing.

This is what I've been doing for the twenty years I've been making a living as a writer.

Anyone can do the same.

8. Be Like a Movie Studio

The successful writers of the pulp and paperback original era, roughly 1920 – 1970, never worked on only one project at a time. While they were writing their main projects they were also developing others to come.

They did not write a book and send it off to the publisher, then sigh and try to think up a new idea.

They had ideas flowing all the time and were ready to go when they typed "The End" on a finished book.

Be like a movie studio. Have several projects "in development." On your breaks from your main writing time, be thinking about what might come next. Have a notebook handy so you can jot down random ideas. Take the ideas that excite you most and begin some random plotting and characterization.

One way to do this is by way of the David Morrell method. Morrell, the author of many bestselling thrillers, happened upon a method inspired by the novelist Harold Robbins. Robbins said he would begin each day talking to his typewriter. And the typewriter would answer him about what to write. (Look, folks, if you call yourself a writer be prepared to be considered eccentric by all your friends. You might as well celebrate it by talking to your laptop).

Anyway, Morrell thought this would be a good method for developing a book. As he explained in an interview with Joanna Penn:

> So I got into thinking, what if I wrote letters to myself, conversations, whatever you want to call them, in which I would, in a conversation with myself, and this is almost schizophrenic, discuss ideas. It would be like, "Well, David, what are we doing here?" and I'd say, "Well, I had this idea for a novel about a guy named Thomas De Quincey," and the other part of me would say, "Well, what's so special about Thomas De Quincey?" and then I would answer that question, and so I'm constantly prodding myself, why is this interesting, who would care, why would you bother doing this? That kind of question. And sometimes

these written conversations have gone on for 10 or 20 single-spaced pages.

The advantage of it is that you don't talk out the idea into the ozone, as you would, say, with a friend or a spouse or a partner or whoever. "Have you got an idea?" "Yes, I've got one, let me tell you about it," and when you're all done, you don't want to write the darn thing. If you've written it on paper, it's a different process, and the advantage of doing this also is that in the long run, let's say, life being what it is, you get sick, or a major catastrophe occurs, well, you can come back to that written conversation and pick it up, and be re-primed, just as when you first wrote it.

This sort of writing can be done in short bursts. There's no pressure. You're just talking to and listening to yourself. You can write two, three pages, stream-of-consciousness, then leave it alone. Come back to it in a week and add to it, see if it still excites you.

You can have several of these letters going on at the same time, much the way a studio has various projects in development. Eventually your mind is going to insist that you give one of these the "green light."

And there's your next book.

4. How to Reach Your Goals

Why set goals? Because you can either control your own destiny or hand it over to circumstance. I'd much rather be acting than reacting. I'd rather have a plan than have time and tide devour me.

Here's how to set and achieve goals:

Decide exactly what you want to accomplish

You must be specific here, and the goal must be something you can make happen.

For example, your goal cannot be to become a #1 *New York Times* bestselling author. Why? Because that's out of your control. You can't force bookstores and readers to buy your book.

What can you do instead? You can do what it takes to become a better writer. You can commit to studying the craft of writing and attending one writers conference a year. You can commit to studying the market and learning what sells. Those are things you can control.

If your dream is to win a golf tournament, you set practice goals. That's what you have within your power.

If you want a certain income, you have to figure out what you can offer that is of value, and then work on that thing. A lawyer, for example, might decide to specialize in an area of law. He can then take courses and study that area thoroughly. He can set up meetings with mentors. He can do things that are within his power.

The results take care of themselves.

Record your goals

Recording your goals means writing them down on paper or typing them into a computer file. I actually like doing both. The act of writing down a goal, placing it on a card I can look at regularly, is a sensory way of getting that goal firmly implanted in my mind.

I have a corkboard program on my computer. On this board I currently have 18 index cards with my writing projects on them. These projects are in various stages, but I can see them every day.

I have another place for my get-off-my-butt goals. And still another document has my long term goals for other parts of my life.

Make plans for your goals

A plan is going to include two things: a deadline and a process.

Deadlines are important because a little time pressure keeps you moving forward. Write down the date you want to see your goal accomplished.

Next, write out a plan of action. What steps are you going to take to realize your goal?

For instance, if my goal is to finish a novel by December 31, I can figure out how many words I'll have to write between now and then. I divide that number by the number of weeks until the deadline. That gives me a weekly quota of words to shoot for.

Also, there might be research time I'll need to include. Maybe I have to go to the location I'm writing about and take some notes and photos. That would be included in the plan.

Just think of all the necessary steps and write them down. Then you can look at exactly where you are and what you need to do next. Check off the steps as you accomplish them. Do this for every goal on your list.

EXAMPLE:

Finish my novel, *The Hound of the Basketballs,* by December 31.
Need to write 6200 words per week.
Research trip to downtown library, micro-film.
Re-read Sherlock Holmes stories.
Schedule freelance editor six weeks ahead.
Second draft finished by Sept. 30.
Beta readers by Dec. 15.
Polish.

Take action every day

Do something, anything, toward your goals, every day. Sure, you're going to have days when things don't go right. But even on days where activity is limited you can find one thing that will be a step forward.

For example, I'm always prepared to "write" when I'm not writing. I have note paper with me and I can jot random thoughts as they occur. I try to keep my "boys in the basement" (the subconscious mind as described by Stephen King) busy in their work.

And when you do, you begin to feel enormous confidence. That, in turn, will motivate you to more action.

You'll be a perpetual goal-achieving machine.

Study, lean and grow in your goal areas

The best way to predict the future is to create it. You do that by study.

Set aside at least one hour a week for reading and studying in a particular area of your craft.

We expect brain surgeons to keep up on the medical journals. Why should it be any different for you (aside from the fact that when you make a mistake no one dies)?

Create self-study programs and put into practice what you learn. There is a feeling of tremendous empowerment when you follow the step outlined in this chapter. You will feel yourself getting stronger. You will look marvelous.

It is sometimes said that the way a writer learns to write is by writing. That strikes me as utterly simplistic, like saying the way a golfer learns to golf is by golfing.

If a wannabe golfer grabs some clubs and just starts hacking, he's going to do nothing but damage to good grass. What he needs is someone to show him how to grip a club, the fundamentals of a good swing, some practice drills and so on. He has to learn to putt and chip, and that doesn't just happen as if a fairy godmother dinked you with her wand.

Paying a teaching professional for lessons is a better idea.

Then you have to play on some small par 3 courses, get your bearings, get some confidence. You have to visit the driving range and ingrain your good habits.

The teaching pro can watch you and help correct mistakes.

It takes a long time to get the hang of that stupid game (I say so in love, because I did finally figure it out).

So it is with writing.

To make it as a writer you need to be two things: systematic and relentless.

Your *system* is your process, the things you do on a regular basis.

Being *relentless* means you never give up. No matter what the setbacks or obstacles, you just keep moving forward.

These are the subjects of the next two chapters.

5. Keys to a Winning System

To have the best shot at making a living as a writer, you need to set up a systematic approach to producing quality work. Here are my own non-negotiables:

Quota

I've already covered this, but I want to emphasize it again. The single greatest piece of writing advice I ever got was to write to a quota. I got it at the beginning of my journey and it's the only way I can account for the number of books and articles I've managed to produce over the years.

I've heard some people balk at writing to a quota. They argue that you can't force art, that there are rhythms to creativity that are not to be tampered with, and that not meeting a quota can lead to discouragement.

Let me first say something about the last point. If missing a quota is enough to discourage you, don't even attempt to write for a living. Write for something else — pleasure, expression, your family.

Writing for a living takes risk, guts and relentlessness. It means not letting little things discourage and dissuade you.

This profession is not for the delicate. You have to develop, as David Eddings once said, "calluses on your soul."

As to the other arguments against quotas, I contend the truth is the very opposite. Writing to a quota strengthens your imagination and expands your craft.

Even if your quota is low in comparison to full-time writers, go for it. Being consistent is what matters. Remember, a page a day is a book a year. Authors who have managed to do that year after year are considered prolific.

Self-study

Along with the regular production of words you need a systematic study of the craft of writing. These are the two train tracks on your journey to writing success. They run right alongside each other, off into the distance.

When I decided I wanted to write thrillers, I went down to my local used bookstore and filled up on John Grisham, Stephen King, Dean Koontz and others. I started reading these books with a pen in my hand, underlining things that jumped out at me. Then I'd ask myself questions.

Why am I compelled to turn the page?

Why do I like this character?

How did this neat twist come about?

Why did this paragraph grab me?

41

Why did he use italics here?

Why do I like this dialogue?

And so on.

At the same time I was devouring Writer's Digest books and magazine. Lawrence Block was the fiction columnist at the time, and I looked forward to his monthly stint as if it were a sacred page. Later, I did the same with Nancy Kress, who took over for Larry.

And then, remarkably, I became the WD fiction columnist myself—which always makes me shake my head in delighted wonder.

I still have binders filled with old WDs, highlighted and indexed.

I bought books on writing and gobbled them up, too. My several bookshelves of these tomes are like a neighborhood of old friends. I love taking out the random volume and just reading over my yellow highlighted portions.

My philosophy was, and still is, that if I can get just one new idea or tip, or get a fresh take on something I already know, it's worth it.

In twenty-five years of purchasing writing books, I can only think of two that I got nothing out of. That's a pretty good record.

In addition to the general study I've described, periodically focus on a specific area you need to improve.

For example, there are seven critical areas of fiction craft: plot, structure, scenes, character, dialogue, voice, and theme. By isolating them this way, you can design a self-study program specific to your needs.

When I was a few books into my traditional publishing career, I had an editor tell me my plotting was strong but my characterizations were weak.

So I set up a six month program for myself.

First, I selected several of my writing craft books that dealt with characters.

Next, I took out several novels that I'd read with truly memorable characters, and bought a few that I'd heard had the same.

Finally, I set aside time for writing exercise. When I read about a technique or saw something that worked in a novel, I practiced it. I'd write practice scenes or sometimes single pages.

And, of course, I'd apply what worked for me in my main writing projects.

Does all this sound like a lot of work? Good, because it is. Writing for a living is not something that's going to fall in your lap. If you truly want to do this, you have to get used to applying what my friend Clare Langley-Hawthorne calls "bum glue" — that which secures your butt to the chair.

Getting Feedback

Authors need outside eyes to look at their stuff. We are the least objective when it comes to our own work.

The two ways to get feedback are with beta readers (non-professionals who read well and can offer good notes) and freelance editors.

How do you find beta readers? You look around. You start with friends who you know are good readers and will pledge to give you an honest opinion.

Try them out. Gift them a Starbucks or Amazon card for their troubles.

Drop the ones who don't work out and recruit new ones with each book. Gradually you'll build up a team you can count on.

And how do you find freelance editors? You need to be careful. The downsizing in the trad-pub world, and the unleashing of digital product, has resulted in a plethora of editors hanging out shingles. No one is licensing them. No one is checking their bona fides.

You have to do that, or you're ripe for disappointment and even a scam.

One website monitoring these is Writer Beware. In a post titled "Bait-and-Switch for Self-Published Authors" it says, in part:

> This isn't a new problem: Writer Beware has been receiving complaints about unqualified editors (both freelance and, unfortunately, employed by small presses) for almost as long as we've been in existence. But the boom in self-publishing has really given it legs. Scammers, con artists, and predators go where the opportunity is--and right now, there is huge opportunity in self-publishing. From small-time operators like FauxReader trying to rip off one author at a time, to big corporations peddling dreams that relieve thousands of authors of cash (*cough* Author Solutions *cough*), the danger is everywhere.

Self-published authors are subject to literary schemes, scams, and cons. Be careful out there. Verify credentials, don't settle for unskilled service providers even if they're cheaper or you like them personally, and beware out-of-the-blue solicitations.

The best way to find a good freelance editor is by referral. Ask writers whose work you admire who they use for editing. If possible, get them to introduce you.

Set up a test edit. Most freelancers will give a one or two page sample of how they work.

Do some comparison shopping, to get a feel for relative costs. But don't shirk on this. A good editor is usually worth the extra bucks.

Critique Groups

Bestselling novelist P.J. Parrish wrote about her critique group's procedure at the writing blog, Kill Zone.

> We meet every two weeks at a Starbucks but in the week prior we send each other our 10 pages. We each then read and "red pencil" our comments on the pages. We use Word's TRACK CHANGES function....
>
> Why just 10 pages at a time? Well, too much makes you skim over surfaces. You can really focus down on a book's problems if you take it in small bites.
>
> What things? We try not to nitpick and line-edit. That's for second and third

drafts and hopefully copy editors. What we try to help each other with is the Big Picture. Where the plot is going into the ditch, where the character development is lacking, and what — and this is important — to the cold eye seems confusing. But we try to stay flexible. We made an exception to our 10-page rule last week for one of our members. She is struggling with a very complex thriller. Her plot had become a hydra-beast and she wanted help simplifying it. So she gave us a concept and we went from there.

Parrish finishes her advice with the following, well worth your consideration:

1. Make a commitment. You'll get only as good as you give. If you join up, be willing to spend whatever time it takes helping the others with their WIPs. Nobody likes the guy who shows up at the party empty-handed, drinks all the good booze and sits in the corner with nothing to say.

2. Be tough but kind. The best editors I've had always know how to make revision letters sound like they are really praise letters. They always tell you what you did brilliantly before they smack you upside the head and tell you where you royally screwed up.

3. Don't get defensive. We are all soft-shelled about our writing but if you can't take constructive criticism, don't join a group. Hell, don't even try to be

a real writer for that matter. At our last session, I got defensive about fried pickles. My hero Louis orders a basket of fried pickles. It was one throwaway line but one of my critique buddies wanted more about the pickles. (It's hard to explain but she was right.) I spent five minutes trying to justify why I didn't want to write more about those friggin pickles. Later, I realized it had nothing to do with pickles and everything to do with me being prickly.

4. Don't ever say "Yeah, but..." This is a variation on No. 3. One of your critique mates says, "I can't figure out what is going on in this scene where the guy is stealing the fried pickles." And you say, "Yeah but if you just wait until chapter 26, it will all be explained." If someone is confused by what you've written you should listen to them. Misdirection is a great writer's tool. But it is not the same as confusion.

5. Don't get depressed. Having folks tell you what is wrong with your story is not easy to hear. But a good critique group can be really inspiring. It can teach you that all writers struggle, that first drafts are never meant to be perfect, and that you can, despite what all the demons in your head are whispering, fix it.

Re-Engineering

Once a year take a day to review your system. Determine if it is delivering the results you seek. See if you need to make any changes.

If you do, remember to commit them to writing. The act of writing things down gets your brain in gear and gives you confidence.

As management guru Peter Drucker puts it, "Knowledge has to be improved, challenged, and increased constantly, or it vanishes."

6. How to Stay Relentless

Just as important as the systematic production of words and improvement of craft is the mental side of the professional writer. Because to make it you're going to need a store of resilience, a reservoir of fortitude and a drive.

There will be many times you want to quit. As Andre Debuse once said, it's very easy to quit during the first ten years.

Years is a key word.

When I was in college I wrote a letter to a novelist I admired, Darryl Ponicsan, author of *The Last Detail*. He wrote back a nice letter of advice, which finished, "Be prepared for an apprenticeship of years."

Knowing this is going to save you a lot of discouragement. A writing business takes time and patience and rarely takes off in only a few years. It can happen, but don't bet on it.

Determine right now that you are in this for the long haul. And that means writing until you die.

Are you going to do that?

Good. Then let's continue.

Get a PHD

No, not a doctoral degree. I mean a PHD attitude: Poor, Hungry and Driven.

So many of the writing successes of the twentieth century were of this manner. Writers struggling in near poverty but so driven to succeed they just would not stop.

William Saroyan was such a writer. He spiked his rejection slips to his wall until there were so many the spike could not contain them. The first story he sold, the one that made him famous, was about a starving young writer who dies.

I'm telling you, you've got to be relentless.

When you are, it gives you a feeling of power. You're never going to give up and no one's going to stop you.

Remember, this is a mental attitude. I believe in strong and positive thinking. You have to be able to turn it on when you need it. But you also have to control it, like an athlete coming off the field. When he's on the pitcher's mound, Clayton Kershaw is in a focused, intense, one-track zone. When he comes off and hits the shower, he relaxes. The next day he begins preparations for his next start.

Get yourself into a fighting mood when you write and plan and set goals and take action.

Overcome Discouragement

You should know this: the writing life is not for those who seek a steady stream of positive vibes. There is always something happening that can rob you of your joy. And some of that is self-inflicted, like an obsession with comparing yourself with other writers.

Case in point. On a discussion site some time ago a writer posted about deep depression setting in after the launch of her self-published, debut novel. She talked about having it edited, having beta readers who liked it, having an "awesome cover." She confessed she was out of whack over getting several negative reviews on Amazon. It was driving her nuts. She didn't know what to do.

If I had a chance to talk with this author, I would say you have to do four things.

First, face the truth. The truth is sometimes hard, but until you deal with it you can't move forward.

In this case, the truth is that the cover is not "awesome," the title is weak and the reviews are honest because *the writing and plotting are not yet strong enough.*

Which means, you have to keep growing as a writer. Sorry, but you can't expect your first book to break out. Most don't, even if they really *are* good. Self-publishing success usually comes only after several books that are *quality reads.*

Second, keep writing. When discouragement hits you, as it will, let it hurt for an hour, but that's it. Then write something, anything, even if it's just a journal entry or a grocery list. Start a new story or work on a current project. You are a writer, first and always, and no one can stop you.

Third, take some time off. After you've written something go do something fun. Get together with friends. See a movie. Shop. Ride a bike. Play Frisbee with a dog. Curl up with a book. Listen to a Beethoven symphony (the "music bath" used to be a highly recommended remedy for the doldrums). Take a whole day if you have to.

Fourth, get in the habit of gathering inspirational writing quotes to refer to in down times. Here are a few to get you started:

"Don't give up. I don't think any other advice works. Writing is one of those things where you just have to do it. There will be far more people to discourage you than to encourage you. The time never comes to you, the inspiration doesn't come to you. You just sit down and do it." – James Lee Burke

"When the last dime is gone, I'll sit on the curb with a pencil and a ten-cent notebook, and start the whole thing all over again." – Preston Sturges

"The best way to predict the future is to invent it." – Alan Kay

"To be a writer, you have to write. Not like it's your job, and not like it's your love. You have to write like it's your holy chore, you have to write like you are compelled from above and within and without and with everything that you are. You have to write *bad* stories, you have to write *cowboy* stories, you have to write period pieces and opinion essays and speeches, and plays, and stuff you wouldn't show your mother and don't wanna see *yourself,* but you can't stop. If you can stop, ever, if you can stop writing, or thinking about writing, or planning what you'll be writing as soon as you get in the hot seat, if you can stop that for even *ten minutes,* you're not a writer. You're a person who can type pretty." – Harlan Ellison

"Be who you are and say what you feel, because those who mind don't matter, and those who matter don't mind." – Dr. Seuss

Discouragement is part of the writer's life. But the more you use the above, the less it will hurt you. You can melt down discouragement to the size of a caraway seed and then you can spit it out.

Don't Let Envy or Comparison Get You Down

It's almost automatic that we writers look at who is on the rungs above us and, in doing so, stay constantly anxious about our own position. Noxious things start popping into the mind: *Hey, I'm a better writer than he is. How come he's selling so much better than me? And what about that guy? He was nothing a few years ago when I taught at a conference. Where does he get off getting that advance? And then, of course, there's THAT one, the legend, the guy I admire most, the guy I wanted to be like, and it's pretty clear I'll never reach his level.*

And so it goes. A certain amount of this you might chalk up to the competitive urge, which is not, per se, unhealthy. We need a little of that warrior in us. But if you let it fester you'll be cooked.

Comparison is death to a writer. There are always going to be writers doing better than you., so why let your mind make a federal case out of it?

Envy is also pointless, though it seems to be an occupational hazard with writers.

Don't let these mental hiccups stop you.

Writing is the best antidote. Get back to work, look at the page in front of you, and nail it.

When you're not writing, learn to nurture gratitude. It is the great secret to happiness. You're unpublished? Be grateful you have the ability to learn the craft. Be grateful for new opportunities in the e-world. Your critique group getting you down? Be grateful for the people in your life who love you. Dogs and cats count, too.

And sprinkle in a little Stoic wisdom. Epictetus (55 – 135 A.D.) said, "There is only one way to happiness and that is to stop worrying about things which are beyond the power of our will."

Where other writers end up on the success scale is not up to you.

The talent you've been gifted is not up to you.

What is up to you is the work.

So keep working.

Stay healthy

If you want to make a living as a writer, the first thing you have to do is live.

The next thing you have to do is live well, so your mind is free to create and produce the words. When your body is shape, your mind is better off. When your mind is better off, the boys in the basement are active and alert, coming up with ideas and sending them topside. Then, when you get them, you have the energy to produce.

It makes sense, then, to think about a few health-related items. Making a living as a writer is about producing the words. Produce more—and better—words by being as healthy as you can.

Here are some health tips for you to consider:

• Write Standing Up

"Sitting is the new smoking," some medical experts are saying. Writing, in the past, mainly meant sitting on your caboose and putting pen to paper or fingers to keyboard. Still true today, but that is changing.

Many office workers are switching to standing desks. A lot of writers, too. You might be able to fashion your own by what you have at home already. For example, I have four in-out trays stacked on the corner of my desk. I also have a Levenger lap desk. I lay that on top of the trays and place my laptop on it. I should note I also have a Griffin laptop stand that raises it another six inches. In this way, I'm able to have the monitor at slightly below eye level, which is recommended.

If you work at a standing desk, be sure to move around a bit, sway, anything but standing stock still. That's hard on the joints.

You can also get a treadmill desk (!) or an attachment that allows you to place a laptop on a treadmill. Hey, it works for a lot of people!

But if the idea of standing or walking while you work doesn't float your boat, at least do this: stand up every 25 minutes or so and walk around for at least 2-3 minutes. That alone will help reduce the dangers of too much sitting.

• Incorporate Regular Exercise

I'm not going to spend a lot of time on exercise, because the information is everywhere and you know where to find it. The key is finding what works for you and then actually doing it.

I've got a treadmill with an attachment that allows me to put my AlphaSmart (or laptop if I want it) in front of me as I walk. I use slow speeds, of course. The point is this is one step ahead (pun intended) of just standing.

Among the other benefits of exercise for the writer is mood control. "I get depressed when my writing isn't going well," wrote Lawrence Block, "and when I'm depressed I can't write, and so on. If I can make myself continue with my regular exercise routine at such times—even though depression makes me inclined to say the hell with it—my depressions aren't as severe and don't last as long." (Block, Lawrence, *The Liar's Bible: A Handbook for Fiction Writers*)

• Hang Upside Down

You may have heard of a writer by the name of Dan Brown. He's going to break out soon, I'm sure of it. He's the author of *The Da Vinci Code* and *Inferno*, among others. When he was writing his follow-up to *Da Vinci*, *The Lost Symbol*, he was feeling enormous pressure. "The thing that happened to me and must happen to any writer who's had success," he told the *Los Angeles Times*, "is that I temporarily became very self-aware. Instead of writing and saying, 'This is what the character does,' you say, 'Wait, millions of people are going to read this.' ... You're temporarily crippled

... The furor died down, and I realized that none of it had any relevance to what I was doing. I'm just a guy who tells a story."

Dan Brown reportedly deals with this pressure by using gravity shoes. He hangs upside down, letting the blood rush to his head. That helps him relax, and also gives him (he says) plot ideas.

The benefits of inversion (for the back and the brain) are well documented. Why not incorporate it into your writer's routine? I use a Total Gym for inversion, but there are products out there dedicated to just that.

As an alternative (which doesn't help the back, but provides the other benefits), lie on the floor with your feet up on a chair. Close your eyes, breathe deeply, and just relax for ten minutes. If your mind is rushing, visualize the number 50 as bright lights, like on a scoreboard. With each breath, see the number change to 49, then 48 and so on down to 0. Take your time, take it slow.

• Take One Day Off Per Week

I've mentioned this before, but it's important enough to say again. You need to let the brain recharge. Read more on that day, priming the pump. I try not to think about the projects I'm working on. I let the crew take care of all that. If something insistent keeps coming up, I'll make a note to follow up on it.

7. Unlocking Your Creative Genius

Schedule a weekly creativity time. Make it an appointment. Calendar it and keep it. Every week.

If you do, I think you'll find it not only one of the most stimulating things you can do for your writing life, but also just plain fun. And we can all use a little more of that, can't we?

Further, we all have been born with a dab of creative genius. If we learn how to find it, encourage it and let it up for air, it will only grow stronger. And you will never run out of material to write about.

Let me offer you a few suggestions to get you started:

1. Find a nice, comfy, low-stress and public spot

Why public? Because there's scientific research that suggests a little bit of noise and activity going on around you is good for the synapses. That's why I prefer good old Starbucks for my spot (I even have a preferred chair). If you're stuck at home, though, guess what? You can replicate the experience by going to Coffitivity.com. Is the internet great, or what?

Get into a nice relaxed mood with a cup of joe or your favorite sipping beverage and settle in. Make your creativity time at least one-half hour. I usually go at least an hour, because once you start you usually want to continue.

2. Use a pen and paper

I know there are numerous apps out there for creativity. And they're really good, too. For example, the Scrivener folks offer a basic "mind mapping" software called Scapple.

But for me there is nothing like moving a pen across a fresh piece of paper, jotting and doodling and making notes. I can do this faster and draw lines and arrows and whatever else I want. I use a simple wire coil notebook for this. Doesn't matter if it's lined paper. I ignore the lines (which is another way of describing creativity!)

3. Start with a goal

It may seem that goals and creativity are at odds, but that's really not the case. Your creative muscles work best when they are given an objective and then let out to play.

Goals might include:

- Coming up with a new story idea
- Creating original characters
- Plotting a new novel
- Creating some killer scenes

- Writing a rich backstory
- Finding twists and turns for a WIP
- Expanding your style
- Creating a new plan for your writing life

Don't feel like you have to stick with your goal once you begin creating. One of the keys to creativity is that when (not if) your imagination urges you to take a tangent, you go ahead and follow it. Rabbit trails are good for you at this stage!

4. Play a game

With a goal in mind, design a creative game to get your imagination pumping. Here are a few of my favorites:

What if?

You simply start asking yourself What if and listen for answers.

Let's say you want to craft a new character. Look around your coffee house and find an interesting face. Then:

- What if she is having an affair with a politician?
- What if she is a hit woman?
- What if she was once a beauty queen?
- What if she just killed her husband?
- What if she was rejected by Brad Pitt?
- What if she's not really a woman?

Let's say the Brad Pitt one intrigues you. You start to imagine that she is an actress who had a very public affair with a movie star, who ultimately rejected her for a glamorous movie queen.

- What if she is plotting revenge?
- What if she had his child?
- What if she has a mob father who can "take care of business"?

And so on. The more What ifs the better!

First Lines

Another game I love is the first line game. You simply write the most compelling opening line you can think of. Dean Koontz used to do this a lot. One day he was having his own creativity time and was doing first lines. He wrote:

"You ever kill anything?" Roy asked.

He had no idea who Roy was or who he was talking to. But the line grabbed him and his imagination started firing. He wrote a scene, and it involved two boys. It got creepy, and Koontz kept writing. The book became one of his early successes, The Voice of the Night.

I have an entire file of first lines, some of which are really, really good. If I need a new project all I have to do is put a novel under them.

Newspaper Noodling

Riff on a newspaper. Remember those? They come on paper. Remember that? You can actually still buy them. But at a coffee house there's usually a discarded front page someone has left behind. Grab it. Now look at each headline on the front page and make up a plot to go with it.

Here is a headline I picked up recently from the *Los Angeles Times:*

Metrolink Squeezed by Plunge in Riders and Revenue

Doesn't sound real exciting, does it? But that doesn't stop me. As a thriller writer I'm thinking:

What if a dirty politician is hiring stinky homeless people to ride the rails to discourage legit riders? Why would he do such a thing? Who would he kill to protect his secret? What if there's a corporate interest involved? What if this reaches not only the mayor's office, but the governor? Heck, the president!

But what if I write romance? Maybe a hot Metrolink official is fired by the equally hot female mayor ... and then they get stuck on a train together, or the train derails and he saves her ... or she saves him ...

Just let your mind play. After a time, move on to another headline.

Use Writing Prompts

There are a number of places to get writing prompts. Just search for "writing prompts" and you'll find books and blogs aplenty. To give you a jump start, I've provided twenty of my favorites below.

This is another favorite of mine, and is great for both plotters and pantsers who are just starting to work on a book. I take a stack of index cards and a pen and settle into my comfy chair, then start writing scene ideas on the cards. My notes are as minimal as:

- Bar fight at fancy hotel.
- He pushes someone out of a building.
- His father shows up at the worst possible time.
- The villain forces him to listen to his speech.

I'll go until I have thirty or forty of these. Then I shuffle the pack and look for the ones that juice me most. I'll take those cards and work a little more on them. What's the setting? Who are the characters? How can I make something surprising happen here? How does it affect the overall story?

Once this is done, I'll shuffle this smaller stack then choose two cards at random. I'll look at them and see if I can make a connection between them, either by plot point or character.

This exercise inevitably prompts more scene ideas, with more connections. I'll do more cards and more weeding out.

Once I have about thirty scenes I like, I'll ask myself where they might go: Act I, Act II, or Act III? I'm starting to build an outline.

5. Come up with tons of ideas

Creativity experts agree that the best way to come up with great ideas is to generate lots and lots of them, without judgment, then come back later to assess which ones you like best.

Learn to make lists. Long lists of possibilities. Be as crazy as you can be. Most of the time you'll find that the first couple of ideas are clichés or stereotypes. That's how our brains work. For example, if I say "Truck driver," I bet most of you envision a man, kind of burly, maybe with boots and Levis and a baseball cap, etc. Push on past that stereotype: What if it's a short person? Or a woman? Or a short woman? Or a man who wears a tutu when he drives? Keep going!

Here is the nice thing about a weekly creativity session: It trains your imagination. It exercises it, makes it stronger. And that means it will start working for you even when you're not being purposeful about it. Those flashes of inspiration you get in the shower or while you sleep will increase. You'll be a rollicking creativity machine.

So get to it.

Every week.

Writing Prompts

Here are twenty writing prompts to get you started. Follow the instructions without over-thinking. Just write. Later on, come back and see what's pleasing to you. That's how it's done!

Prompt 1

Write for five minutes without stopping, completing this sentence: "I hated it when _____"

Prompt 2

You're at a party. In walks the person you least want to see in the world. Write the scene.

Prompt 3

What is your favorite animal? On YouTube, type in that animal's name. When the results come up, choose the third video and watch it. Now write a page of what the animal is thinking.

Prompt 4

On Google Images, search for "construction worker." Choose a headshot. Now give the character a name. What is the one thing this character has hidden in a closet that he/she doesn't want anyone to ever find? Write a scene where the character comes home to discover a friend hunting through the closet.

Prompt 5

You wake up, walk outside and see no signs of life. Everything appears normal, but there are no people or dogs or squirrels. Write the opening to a story in first-person POV.

Prompt 6

Begin a story with this line: *They threw me off the hay truck about noon.*

Prompt 7

The Most Interesting Man in the World has this career advice: "Find the thing that you're not very good at, then don't do that thing." What is something you're not very good at? Now, write a scene where you are forced to do it.

Prompt 8

A good-looking man walks into a bar and spots a good-looking woman alone. He sits on the stool next to her and says, "Here I am. What were your other two wishes?" Write the scene.

Prompt 9

Do a half hour of research on Blaise Pascal. Write a short essay in middle-school reading level explaining who he was and why he's remembered.

Prompt 10

Make a list of ten things people are obsessed with. Now choose number five on that list. Begin a story with a character demonstrating that obsession.

Prompt 11

What is the thing you fear most? Put that into the character of a child and write a scene about it.

Prompt 12

Write a free form poem (no rhyming) about a boy wanting an orange in a grocery store.

Prompt 13

Choose five childhood memories and title them with a single noun. For example, the time your father took you to the circus would be, The Circus. The time you broke your arm on the side of a pool, The Pool.

Take one of them and write a short scene about the incident, only make it from the POV of a character you make up, a child of the opposite sex.

By the way, Ray Bradbury made a long list of these kinds of nouns and used them over the course of his career as the basis of stories.

Prompt 14

Write a letter to your favorite dead author, asking for writing advice. Then write his or her letter back to you.

Prompt 15

Imagine your Lead character in a room with a large window. He (or she) takes a chair and throws it through the window. What would make him do that? Write that scene.

Prompt 16

Your Lead is being chased through a national monument. Pick a monument and write that scene.

Prompt 17

You are in a graveyard and see a stone that says: Barnaby Luckey, 1809 – 1842. I told you I was sick.

Write a short biography of Barnaby.

Prompt 18

You are transported back in time to the deck of the Titanic on its fateful night. In two hours it will hit the iceberg. Write a story about you trying to get to the captain and stop the tragedy.

Prompt 19

Write this line: "I never should have done that." What is the thing you shouldn't have done? Write two pages without stopping describing why you did it and how you feel about it now. (Note: transport these feelings to the Lead character in your WIP)

Prompt 20

A man walks up to a woman sitting at a bar and says, "You must be my ticket, cause you've got fine written all over you." Write the scene from the POV of the man, then again from the POV of the woman.

8. How to Write More, Faster

There are three kinds of writers in the world: those who can count, and those who can't.

And there are fast writers and slow writers.

Okay, who's measuring? We all have different paces.

There are writers who seem to be able to pound out a book a month. Barbara Cartland made a pretty good living that way, though critics were not enamored of her quality. For Cartland, critical praise was not a high value. She led the life of the well-compensated writer.

In the self-publishing ranks, there are writers making seven-figures, like Joe Konrath, because they are so fast (and, let it be noted, able to tell a story). There are even some making eight figures cranking out the books. Bella Andre is one such writer.

Other writers just don't have that kind of output. Many published authors struggle to put out one book a year.

In the "old days" of publishing, back in the 1950s for example, a writer like Herman Wouk or James Michener could take years between books. But they (and their publishers) knew the books would sell enough to continue making everybody happy.

I'm an advocate of writing as fast *as you comfortably can*. I believe that creativity and flow and your best material come when you can get those words down relatively fast. You take your time when editing, but when you compose, get out of the way and let the words and ideas come.

If you are a slow writer, consider that part of the reason may be fear. You think that if you write too fast your quality will suffer. This is a bias toward control that is a common affliction among writers. You want to assert quality control up front, at the creation stage.

What you need to do is allow yourself to write junk. Don't try to shape every word or page as you write. Dean Koontz is on record as saying he makes each page perfect, editing quite a bit, before moving on to the next. That way lies madness, unless you are Dean Koontz, who writes something like 70 hours a week.

He is a full-time writer. He seems to be doing okay at it.

You have a baseline of production that is a natural fit for you right now. In this chapter I'd like to give you some suggestions for upping your word count without too much disruption to your life or comfort zone.

Write Without Stopping

Try writing a page of your WIP without stopping. Set a timer for five minutes and write, not pausing to edit anything.

Practice this daily. Five minutes of pure writing time.

If you aren't working on a book at the moment, use one of the prompts in Chapter 7 to get you going.

Do this every time you write for at least ten writing sessions. It will then begin to show you the benefits.

First, it will up your raw writing speed.

Second, it will train your imagination to crank out more material at a faster rate.

When you finish your speed writing, take a moment to assess it and find what you like in it. It may be only one sentence, but that may be the gold. Even if you don't find anything you want to keep, this practice is still accomplishing its goal—making you a faster writer.

Try a Dose of Dr. Wicked

There's a cool little program out there that you can use online or download to your computer (for a minimal cost). It's called Dr. Wicked's Write or Die. It lets you set a timed goal for word production. Once you start, you need to keep going or the program issues a loud, obnoxious sound that won't stop until you start typing again.

It's fun. Some writers I know use it daily to "warm up the engines." I've used it when I come to a particularly intense moment in a scene and I want to pour out as much feeling and emotion as I can.

What I produce here is "overwriting," which means I'll go back over it and cull what I find useful for my actual WIP.

Dictate

Most writers today recognize the value of using voice recognition software for at least some of their writing. It takes a bit of getting used to, and the style that emerges may be a bit different than what you produce when typing manually.

But it is great for getting the word count up. I find it best to dictate a minimum of a thousand words at a time, then quickly edit those words for style, punctuation and word choice (you have to watch out for the odd word switch that sometimes happens!)

I also find it helpful to stand when I dictate. I have my computer on a standing desk and a long cord on my microphone. I pace around, close my eyes sometimes, using my arms to make gestures as if I'm playing the role. It opens up different lobes in the brain.

The Nifty 350

At the start of my writing life, dedicated as I was to a daily quota, I found that if I wrote 350 words the very first thing, the whole writing day went better. Pressure was off to some degree. I knew that I could make my quota pretty easily after that.

If you can find a way to write in the morning, make it a goal to get to it first thing. Forget email and social media (the great time sucks) and learn to get your words done. You'll feel better all day.

Find Your Zone

Of course, not everyone is a morning person. But we all have a zone of time when we are most creative. For many writers it's indeed the morning, right after a jolt of java. But others seem to come alive at night, after the day's events are over.

The trick is to find your zone and guard it jealously.

Do everything you can to get to your writing during this time frame. Blast it for all it's worth.

The 200-Word Nightcap

Before you retire for the evening, write 200 more words. You may be tired, you may be groggy, but 200 words is not that hard to do (especially if you've trained yourself in fast writing as suggested above).

Further, writing just before bed gets your subconscious working while you sleep.

In the morning, you can jump right into your Nifty 350 in virtually the same "flow" as your 200-Word Nightcap.

Write in 25-Minute Chunks

Try writing in segments of 25 minutes. When you write, write. Stay focused and productive.

Then take a break.

Lie down with your feet up for ten minutes.

Take a stroll outside.

Move around.

Then come back and do another 25 minutes.

You'll find yourself more productive and more energized.

Use a Spreadsheet to Track Your Words

I've already mentioned this, but I do so again here. Keeping to your quota (remember, what is comfortable for you plus 10% more) is also a motivational tool. When you see the words racking up, you'll be stoked.

On the other hand, if you see the word count falling behind, it should motivate you to speed up.

One tip so you will avoid getting cranky about this: I keep a weekly tally of my words. If one of my weeks goes badly and I'm below my quota, I forget about that week. I don't try to make it up the next week. I throw that bad week out like it's the first waffle of the day. I start fresh with the new week.

Find the Joy

Writing ought to be enjoyable. Not that it's always easy. But when we write we should feel a certain joy in what we're doing. It's magic, after all, to write stories that will capture readers, or books of information that will improve lives.

In each scene or chapter we write, there is a core of joy waiting to be discovered.

For fiction, I find that it's the unexpected. So I have a little acronym: SUES. That stands for "something unexpected in every scene."

I spend time thinking up at least one thing that will be surprising to a reader. It has to surprise me first.

74

It can be a character action, a line of dialogue, an event, a twist, a shock. I'll just wait for my imagination to come up with something, and then I find I'm excited about writing the scene.

For non-fiction, find the benefit in the chapter. The core idea. Think about it until you are convinced of its worth. Find the thing that you most want to share with the readers. If you're excited about it, the odds are they will be, too.

For further tips, check out this viral blog post from author Rachel Aaron, who upped her word count mightily with only a few tweaks:

http://thisblogisaploy.blogspot.com/2011/06/how-i-went-from-writing-2000-words-day.html

9. A Sample Plan

Below is an example of what your written plan might look like. Begin with your vision then set your goals. Finally, take action every day toward your goals.

It's as simple as that. The power is in the doing of it.

Vision Statement

I am a writer of thrillers and paranormal tales that engage readers because they move fast, hit hard and have a touch of humor that comes from my odd sense of the world. I also write books about my passion for fitness. I sell enough books to make a living from my writing.

Goals

This year, I will write one full-length novel (75,000 words) and two novellas (35,000 words each). I will produce a 25,000 word book on the fitness plan that lost me 25 pounds. I also will systematically study the craft of writing with special concentration on my weak areas (dialogue, characterization and theme).

Action steps

- Weekly quota of words: 3,000

- Study time: 3 sessions per week, 1/2 hour per session

- Line up group of beta readers
  * Generate list of names
  * Ask for interest (offer gift card)

- Vet freelance editors, cover designers
  * Ask for recommendations
  * Check internet sources
  * Seek sample edits from top candidates

- Finalize revamped website with sign-up form for emails

- Create social media plan with good ROI (Return on Investment). Research what works best

- Attend the Writer's Digest Conference in August

Now Write Your Own

Using this template, take an hour to write up your own, personal plan. Come back to it tomorrow and revise as you see fit.

Re-visit the plan in 6 months and make any adjustments that are called for.

Then take action.

Be unstoppable.

10. Traditional v. Self Publishing: Which One?

Now it's time for some plain talk about your publishing possibilities. You have three options: traditional, indie, or some combination of both.

Traditional

A brief history. In 1440 a German printer named Johannes Gutenberg unveiled a press that used moveable type to ink impressions on paper. Contrary to myth, he was not inundated with submissions from would-be novelists. But his invention did change the course of literacy and book production forever.

As more and more people learned to read, the demand for books went up. A class of businessmen found out they could make money by producing books and selling them. Other businessmen discovered they could open up shops to sell the books produced by the first class of businessmen.

The whole thing was dependent on people who could actually write things the public would want to read.

The author as professional was born.

Some, like Charles Dickens, did very well.

Most, like Herman Melville, did not. *Moby-Dick* sold dismally during his lifetime. And thus the "commercial failure" was born.

To be a commercial failure meant that your likelihood of getting another contract for a book was extremely difficult.

Just getting into print was extremely difficult, too.

Those who did sometimes managed a pretty good living. Authors as diverse as Ernest Hemingway and Agatha Christie, Thomas Wolfe and Max Brand all got paid good money for their work.

But most authors never made a living from writing alone. And all authors were subjects of the "publishing industry," which was the only game in town.

And that's the way it stayed until November, 2007. That's the month a little company called Amazon introduced a device they called the Kindle.

The years since the Kindle intro have been challenging for traditional publishing. Many economic factors have contributed to this, which are beyond the scope of this book. Suffice to say, as of this writing, the major publishers have coalesced into five companies. I expect that soon it will be four. Perhaps three.

But today there is still a traditional publishing *industry*. And some writers who seek to write for a living would like to do it the "old fashioned way."

For some, making it here represents "validation." A very difficult industry to enter (I sometimes call it "the Forbidden City") giving you the nod means you've "made it." You've proved your worth. Your friends and high school creative writing teacher now know you're a "real writer."

There's nothing wrong with this desire. Just know that it is becoming ever more difficult to get inside the gates of the Forbidden City. That's because the City has to be more risk averse these days. And all new writers represent a risk.

Now let's look at the pros and cons of going exclusively with trad-pub.

Pros

1. Physical book distribution

The network of publishers and bookstores and distributors is still in place. For getting printed books into stores, this system is still the best.

2. A-list career

If a publisher really gets behind a book or an author, a career as a bestselling author might be launched. I'm talking about the kind of careers a Stephen King, Lee Child, Michael Connelly, Janet Evanovich, Nora Roberts all enjoy. In 2013 Dean Koontz made around $80 million. That is virtually impossible outside the walls of the Forbidden City. Even E. L. James, author of the indie sensation *50 Shades of Gray,* did not reach the top of the *Forbes* list of highest paid authors ($95 million in 2013) until Random House picked it up.

3. Production quality

Things like cover design, print layout, editing (in some cases; see below) are all part of the system of production that trad-pub has been doing well for years.

4. Advances

Trad-pub offers authors an advance against royalties. That means money in your pocket before the book appears.

5. A home for literary writing

By and large, so-called "literary" novels do not sell in great abundance when they are self-published. Just what is a literary work? There's not one agreed-upon definition.

Sometimes it's defined by what it is not — it is not genre writing. It is not commercial writing. It is usually more concerned with character psychology and/or style than with straight plot and page turning.

An old pulp writer said it's the difference between "art and beauty" and "cash and carry" prose.

To Kill a Mockingbird would probably not sell a whole bunch today if it came out self-pubbed. Which is why many established authors hope that traditional publishing stays around, so it can nurture and curate this kind of novel in the future.

Cons

1. An A-list career faces extremely long odds

The kind of career that the A-list stars enjoy are rare and subject to a thing called luck (or Providence, or Fate). Very few authors ever make seven, let alone eight, figures a year. Very few authors enjoy the placement of their books in airports and store end caps.

If you want to take those odds, you certainly may. If it does not work out as planned, you may have given several years of your writing life to a publisher who does not renew your contract, and who holds the rights to the books you wrote.

2. Editorial services pared down

Because of the challenge of the digital age, traditional publisher have been forced to streamline their staffs. The nurturing editors of the past, the ones who could spend a lot of time with writers helping them get better, are virtually all gone now.

3. Stringent contract terms

In return for being allowed inside the Forbidden City, the publisher is going to ask you to accede to some very tight contract terms. Right now, the standard contract tops out at 25% of net. No author really thinks that's fair, but it's the price you pay for getting inside the gates.

You are also likely to be asked to give up your rights to ever publish the material yourself, unless rights are reverted to you. But reversion of rights clauses are getting ever tighter because having a book remain "in print" is so easy.

Further, you're likely to see a non-compete clause that restricts your ability to self-publish other material.

4. A long time for a book to appear

It takes about eighteen months, on average, for a book you contract with a publisher to make it to the bookstore shelves.

5. Shelf space is shrinking

The brick-and-mortar bookstore business is in a world of hurt. The large bookstore chain Borders went bankrupt in 2011. Barnes & Noble has been closing stores at the same time it is shrinking book shelf space in favor of other items.

Small, independent bookstores are hanging in there in some places, but they are not ordering a lot of books.

Nor are the big box stores, like Costco and Wal-Mart.

For a new book to gain traction in print it needs to be seen. But the real estate for print books is disappearing at an alarming rate.

Self-Publishing

When ebooks started taking off in 2008-09, the traditional publishing industry saw this as a fabulous new way to move units. No printing costs! No warehousing! Almost pure profit!

But what they didn't see coming was the tidal wave behind them.

Because along about 2009 a crop of authors began to emerge who were publishing directly to the Kindle store. Amazon was offering an incredible deal: a 70% return on sales!

What? How could this be?

Oh, it be.

Soon some authors no one had ever heard of started raking in very big bucks. Amanda Hocking, for example, was a young writer of paranormal fiction who was selling scads of ebooks and raking in the dough.

It did not take long for other writers to follow suit. A traditionally published author named J. A. Konrath took the plunge and soon became a leading voice for this new outlaw crowd.

Traditional publishing, meanwhile, as well as most literary agents, were looking askance at these success stories and calling them anomalies. No serious writer, no writer who wanted a real career, would ever stoop to self-publishing, which was only one step above selling your body on the street on Saturday night.

And then a *New York Times* bestselling writer named Barry Eisler turned down a half a million bucks from his publisher to go all-in with self-publishing.

At the time I called this The Eisler Sanction. I said it was a tipping point.

Time has proved this to be true. Since Eisler's move self-publishing has exploded, with more and more authors skipping the trad world and going right to indie. And more and more are making a full-time living this way.

Now let's consider the pros and cons:

Pros

1. Control of content and speed of publication

Whenever indie writers are polled or informally questioned, almost always they cite the control factor as the biggest plus in self-publishing. You decide when something is ready to publish. And then you decide when to publish.
No waiting.

2. You get paid every month

One of the biggest complaints with traditional publishing is that the writer only gets paid every six months—provided his books have earned out their advance. And often the royalty statements read like code from the intercepted German messages of World War I.
Self-publishing writers get paid each month, and the sales statements are straightforward and easy to analyze.

3. You cannot be dropped by your publisher

You never have to stop. You don't have to fire yourself. You can keep on going as long as you want. You don't need permission to do this.

Cons

1. You take all the risks

There is no one sharing the expenses with you. You will have to shoulder all the risks of bringing a book to market. That includes up-front costs for editing and design. The good news here is those costs are not prohibitive.

2. It usually takes many books to get established

The name of the self-publishing game is quality and quantity. You need to provide both. It's not just the number of books you have out there — they also have to be so good readers will talk about them and want to see more from you.

If you are hoping to strike gold with one book, you are likely to be severely disappointed.

A Bit of Both

The blended writer (sometimes called a *hybrid*) is one who has ongoing traditional contracts while, at the same time, produces self-published works. Those works may be books that were once published by a traditional publisher and to which the writer has had the rights returned (the author's *backlist.)*

Some authors publish new work themselves to help support their traditional books. These are usually short stories or novellas, designed to get new readers interested in the trad books.

In either case, the author must make sure his self-published work does not run afoul of a publishing contract's non-compete provision.

So what about an author who self-publishes as a way to get noticed, build an audience and perhaps gain the interest of a traditional publisher?

It's happened. Hugh Howey famously made a big splash with *Wool,* which led to his association with a top agent, which led to a favorable deal with a big publishing house. Editors at houses now keep an eye on bestselling self-pubbers. It's a low-risk way to find authors who already have a readership.

If you ever get to the point where a traditional house comes knocking at your door, don't jump at the first offer. Get someone to help you assess your possibilities.

Note, there are small publishing companies popping up all over the place. These companies vary in quality. There is a risk in assigning your rights to such a company. I've seen small enterprises go belly up, stop their fiction lines, get sold, get lost, act incompetently or even viciously (e.g., using litigation to intimidate authors and shut down critics).

I'm not saying you shouldn't go with a small publisher, but be very cautious and check them out thoroughly.

Avoid what's called "vanity publishing." These are imprints that promise all sorts of benefits in return for very steep fees. Sometimes these imprints are associated with major publishing houses. That may make you think it's a way to get noticed by the "big leagues." In reality, it's just a way for the big company to generate revenue.

Do not pay to be published. I'm not talking about the costs you incur yourself as you prepare your book, or those fees associated with a *distributor* (like Smashwords or BookBaby).

I'm talking about the hundreds or thousands of dollars a vanity imprint will want to collect from you.

To help you through the traditional publishing thicket, you can partner with an agent, who will represent you in return for 15% of your proceeds. It's difficult, though not impossible, to find an agent to represent you to the traditional publishing world. It's easier if you already have an offer in hand.

An alternative is to hire an Intellectual Property lawyer (one who specializes in book contracts) and pay a flat fee for a review of the offered contract. In that case, you keep all the royalty income.

My advice to all traditionally published writers who want to self-publish is to talk about it. Have a discussion with your agent. Come up with a strategy for talking to the editor at the publishing house. Pitch your self-publishing venture as a way to build readership for the trad books, and not as something that's going to keep you from doing your best work for the house. That's what you owe them. That's why they've paid you an advance.

11. How to Go Traditional

Going for a traditional contract is a little like preparing for a long battle. You'll need strategy, tactics, killer writing and a presence on the internet.

The risks of publishing a new writer are greater now than ever. Big and small publishers therefore take an ever-closer look at who they take on.

What they want is someone who will be a reliable pro, produce good work book after book, and have a quality public persona.

Which means a sharp website and positive social media profile.

You will be Googled.

Any editor or agent who is looking to take you on is going to look you over, digitally speaking.

One agent put it this way:

> I always Google. Always. Usually at the query stage. I'm looking for how that person presents him- or herself online. Are sites updated? Are they sloppy or professional? Are they complaining about agents and

publishing? (That's a red flag.) I'm also looking at whether I can find the person at all. Sometimes I can't, and that's almost always an instant pass.

Plan your assault on the Forbidden City well in advance.

You're going to need a completed novel.

It's got to be the very best you can do. Put it through the grinder.

Then begin.

Agents

If you desire to go after a traditional contract, a good agent is invaluable. Note the key word, *good*. My axiom is this: A bad agent is worse than no agent. So you must do your due diligence in sorting out the wheat from the chaff. Get recommendations and check the client lists on the agency's website. Do some research on some of those clients (there will usually be a link to the author's website). Find out what kind of career they're having. What publishing houses have they signed with?

Of course, the more popular the author names, the harder it will be to get into that agency. Even if you did, you would be a small fish in a big pond.

That's why it is sometimes better for the new writer to sign with an agent who is just starting out. *Writer's Digest* magazine (which you should subscribe to) regularly runs a list of new agents and what kind of books they're looking for. Writer's Digest Books publishes an annual guide to literary agents.

Some warnings:

By no means pay any up-front fees to an agent. No reading fees, no editing fees. Cross such agents off your list.

Other nefarious practices might be requiring you to pay for editing or referring you to an editorial service. In the latter case the agent is probably getting finders fee of some kind (or may even own an interest in the service).

How long should you wait after querying an agent? They're busy, so give them eight weeks. At that point, send a simple follow up email to see if they've received your material.

Three months is long enough to wait.

Can you query more than one agent at a time? Yes. And you should. Because it takes so blinking long to hear from most of them.

Writer's Digest Books publishes the definitive *Guide to Literary Agents* every year. Be sure to have it on hand when you start your journey to find one. You might also consider attending a conference where agents are in attendance and receive short pitches.

Make a list of six agents who you think are a good fit. Follow their submission guidelines, which you'll find on their websites or in the *Guide*. Then simultaneously submit to them. You do not have to tell them that you are doing so. A good agent will know authors do this.

Because this is a *business*. You are entitled to conduct yourself as a business.

But what if you get more than one offer?

Pop some champagne.

Now *you* are in the driver's seat. Choose the one you want most and send a nice Thank You note to the one you turned down.

Never burn bridges. You're a professional and you will begin to gather a reputation. Make it a good one.

Do you need an agent at all? Some writers have been able to propose directly to a publishing house via an acquisitions editor. This is best done if you've met the editor at a conference and you've been invited to submit.

However, you can certainly try, via a query, to interest an editor at a house. Just be sure it's the right editor and house, and that they publish the kind of books you write.

Do not ever send a query to a big publisher addressed to: *To whom it may concern* or *Acquisitions Editor.*

Contract Issues

If you want to go traditional, that means you are going to be signing contracts. You need to have a modicum of knowledge about what such contracts might hold for you. You need to be aware of potential pitfalls and risks, because publishers and their lawyers have been drafting contracts for hundreds of years.

You haven't.

So do some learning. A good place to start is with *The Writer's Legal Companion* by Brad Bunnin and Peter Beren. It was last updated in 1998, but since it deals with traditional book contracts the information is still largely valid. You can easily find a used copy to purchase, or perhaps at your local library.

Here I will give you a heads-up on some of the key contract terms to watch for.

If an agent offers to represent your work, you will probably be asked to sign a contract. The contract will give the agent the authorization to shop your work, negotiate contracts, collect the monies from publishers and receive a 15% commission on the payments.

The key provisions in an agency contract concern the term of the agreement, termination rights, payment of expenses, and exactly what work the agent is entitled to receive a commission on.

A) Term: The contract may ask for a one-year term. The agent will want a chance to try to sell your work, which takes time. Once the year expires, what happens? If you're pleased with the relationship, you'll want it to continue, *but not for another fixed term.*

Instead, the language should be something like, "Upon expiration of the term of this contract, the authorization granted in this Agreement shall continue unless and until it is terminated according to the terms in paragraph ___."

B) Termination: A standard clause gives either side termination rights with 30 days' notice. That's fair. Also fair is a standard clause that gives the agent the right to continue to collect and disburse any money that comes in on contracts with publishers that remain in force.

What if you have a proposal or manuscript with an agent and he's been shopping it around, and then you terminate the contract? If you shop the project yourself, or through another agent, and get a contract, the original agent might assert the right to a commission. This is more likely if the agent has operated as something of an editor for the project, giving you notes and suggestions which you have incorporated.

Be sure there is language in the contract (under the clause that specifies what the agent is entitled to receive) to this effect: "Agent shall be entitled to receive payments and royalties from completed contracts only, and only so long as said contracts remain in force."

C) Expenses: Some old-school contracts charged the client for certain expenses, such as making copies, postage, and long-distance calling. Because there are so few paper copies used anymore, and email and phone expenses (except for overseas calling) are virtually nil, this clause should be limited to "extraordinary expenses necessary for representing Client's work." The clause should specify: "Before such expenses become payable, they must be discussed with and agreed to by Client."

D) Payment: For any contract that is signed, the agent is entitled to receive a 15% commission. The publisher pays the agent, the agent sends a check to the author, less the commission.

So what happens if a publishing relationship comes to an end and the rights to publish the book are reverted to the author...and the author self-publishes the book. Does the author owe the agent 15% again?

The answer should be no, but the contract language may not be clear. An agency contract may have language like the following: "Agency will be the Agent-of-Record for all Projects sold and will irrevocably retain 15% of all income derived from the Project."

Uh-oh. The way that language reads it can be interpreted as entitling the agent to a commission as long as your project makes money, even if it is self-published.

Instead, you should insist that the right to collect money only pertains to the *contracts* the agent has negotiated for you. Thus, if a contract is no longer in effect, you have the right to do what you want with your book. Repeating the sample language from the termination discussion, above, you should have something like this: "Agent shall be entitled to receive payments and royalties from completed contracts only, and only so long as said contracts remain in force."

In recent years, many authors have reached agreements with their agents for self-publishing services. In return for 15%, the agency handles all the technical details of getting your book back to market. This would be similar to you publishing your books through Smashwords or some other service that keeps a percentage of royalties.

Do not obligate yourself to this kind of relationship in the agency contract. You can then decide if you want to go ahead with such a deal, or do it on your own and keep the 15% (which lasts for the life of the book, mind you) for yourself.

The contracts being offered by both big and small publishers used to be fairly uniform. But with all the upheaval in the digital world, that is no longer the case. More than ever an author needs to be aware of what is likely to show up in a contract, and what terms should be a "deal breaker."

A good agent will discuss these terms with you.

On some occasions, especially with smaller publishers, authors have been able to score deals on their own. If that happens with you, invest in the expert eye of a good Intellectual Property attorney, one that has experience with publishing contracts.

You may have some hunting around to do to find such a lawyer, but it's worth every penny when you do. Seek out other writers' recommendations should this need arise.

The big terms of a publishing contract are: royalties, non-compete, duty to publish, and reversion of rights. All the terms are important, of course, but these are the ones that have the most lasting effect.

A) Royalties: The publisher is going to set royalty rates for both print and ebooks. For print, there are standard ranges for the various formats (hardcover, trade paper, mass market). These have slight variations from publisher to publisher. They may be based on the retail price of the book or the net income.

A standard range for a retail contract looks like this:

Hardcover editions:

10% of the retail price on the first 5,000 copies

12.5% of the retail price on the next 5,000 copies

15% of the retail price on all copies thereafter

Trade paperback:

7.5% of the retail price

Mass market:

8% of the retail price on the first 150,000 copies

10% of the retail price on all copies thereafter

As far as ebooks, that is a subject of some controversy at the moment. As soon as ebooks became a reality, all of the big publishing houses held to a 25% royalty for their authors. Seems like quite a coincidence, doesn't it? I think more than one three-martini lunch was involved, but that's just me.

Anyway, authors and their agents began to ask if that was fair. After all, there is no cost to printing or warehousing an ebook. Wouldn't it be fairer to split this 50/50?

Publishers responded that they still had overhead (yeah, in Manhattan!) and related development costs.

As of this writing, the 25% is still pretty solid across the board. (The authors who get much better terms here are the A-list writers, the mega-sellers, who have the leverage to negotiate).

Try to negotiate this up to 50%. If they won't budge, maybe they'll at least come up to 35%. If they hold the line at 25%, you must make the decision whether or not that is a deal breaker. This should be thoroughly discussed with your agent *before* the agent goes shopping your project.

B) Non-Compete: This is a huge issue for writers now, and has even been the cause of some vexatious litigation — by both publishers and authors.

First, let's consider the reason for this clause. It generally holds that the author will not publish, or cause to be published, another work (from himself or another publisher) that will "compete" with the book the publisher is putting out there.

The publisher takes a risk with an author, puts up capital (in the form of advance and production costs) with the hope of return. A significant part of the return is from bookstores (remember those?) Bookstores do not want to stock competing titles from the same author during the same season.

Thus, the standard non-compete was to keep John Grisham from publishing *The Firm* with one publisher and *The Pelican Brief* with another, and having them both come out at the same time. The books would "cannibalize" each other, so the saying goes. One, or more likely both, publishers could be harmed by this.

Here's another reason publishers want this clause. Suppose Publisher is coming out with your debut thriller, and pricing it as a $14.99 trade paperback, and a $9.99 ebook. But, at the same time, you bring out a self-published thriller and price it at $3.99 in digital and the same $14.99 through CreateSpace. And then you unleash your social media marketing efforts to emphasize the book that's bringing you more money per unit (i.e., your self-pubbed effort).

That's not cricket. You are hurting Publisher's investment in you. That's why the non-compete clause exists.

On the other hand, publishers can truly turn this clause into a nightmare for the author. It can prohibit an author from publishing anything of any length that might compete. It can virtually rule out any self-published work, unless permission is secured from the publisher.

Everyone, including the publishers, know that the non-compete clause is hated by authors and tolerated by agents. There has thus been some movement on the negotiating of this clause.

My view is that it should be limited and specific. It should pertain only to the genre and/or series you have been contracted for. Here are two sample clauses:

> For six months from the date of publication of the Work, Author will not publish or authorize to be published, in either print or digital media, any work greater than sixty-thousand words in the thriller genre.

> For six months from the date of publication of the Work, Author will not publish or authorize to be published, in either print or digital

media, any work greater than sixty-thousand words about the series character featured in the Work.

Publishers are now savvy about the value of short form work being made available as ebooks prior to the release of a new title. It generates interest. It builds readership.

You should retain the rights to these shorter works and publish them yourself. You and your agent need to discuss this up front with the publisher. In fact, pitch them a plan to follow this very strategy.

If the publisher declines to negotiate the non-compete and you don't have any desire to self-publish, you can go ahead and sign the thing.

But remember your mind might change. So do all you can to get the limited non-compete.

C) Duty to Publish: Many publishing contracts say that the publisher only has the duty to publish a book they deem "acceptable." That leaves them a lot of leeway. Suppose you have a three-book contract and they don't like the returns on the first and second books. You send them book #3, and maybe you think it's your best. But the publisher doesn't want to publish it now. They might find a way to deem it unacceptable. The discretion is all theirs.

On the other hand, a publisher should not have to publish a piece of crap.

So try to negotiate a clause that states before rejecting a manuscript you, the author, shall receive detailed editorial notes from the publisher and shall have the right to submit another draft within an agreed upon deadline.

D) Right to Terminate and Reversion of Rights: In the old days, the return of rights to an author usually depended on a physical book going "out of print." OOP was defined in certain ways, usually referring to how much stock was left in the warehouse, and whether or not the book was available through the publishers catalogue.

All that has changed now, due to two things: ebooks and print-on-demand (POD). An ebook is forever, so a book can be said to be "in print" forever. And the warehousing of physical books isn't necessary because they can now be printed in any quantity simply by placing an order with the POD company.

Thus, rights reversion should be based upon the payment of royalties. Try for a contract that states your book must earn royalties of $1,000 during a six-month royalty period. If the book does not earn that, it shall be considered out-of-print and the rights to the book will "automatically" revert to you.

This clause will be the subject of negotiation. The publisher will want to get that royalty number down as low as possible. Also, they may insist that reversion of rights must be requested in writing.

The first part is the most important. Decide what "floor" you are willing to settle for. Personally, I wouldn't let it go below $500.

The Novel Proposal

The three parts of the novel proposal are:
- the introduction

- the synopsis
- your first three chapters

A great intro is like a firm handshake. It makes the recipient want to see what you're all about. A bad letter is like a fish handshake or a Hello with garlic breath.

Make your intro no longer than three paragraphs.

Paragraph 1 is a plot paragraph. You've already got it. It's your elevator pitch! (See Chapter 14 for instruction on writing the elevator pitch).

Paragraph 2 is the "who you are" paragraph. Don't gild the lily. Just put down your basic background and any literary awards or training you've received. If you are writing about your specialty (say, a lawyer writing a legal thriller), of course mention that, too.

A synopsis should read like your book description on steroids. Two pages max. It's the sizzle.

And then your first three chapters (some guidelines may ask for your first five or ten pages). Why the first three instead of just any three?

Because if you send some middle chapters, the agent or editor will wonder what's wrong with your opening.

The opening is what hooks readers. Editors and agents want to know you can do that.

By the way, the part of your proposal that is usually read first is page one of your sample chapters. Why? Because it saves time. If you can't write, the reader doesn't have to bother with the rest of the package.

What about a chapter-by-chapter outline? Submit that only if it is specifically requested. Otherwise, don't bother. There is no way to make an outline of chapters read well. Some novelists look at a book on proposal writing and mistakenly believe that the requirements of a fiction proposal are the same as a non-fiction book. Not so. Outlines are essential to the nonfiction proposal. They are fine in that context because they are giving hard information about the sections of the book.

But fiction is about story, and chapter outlines do not make for compelling narrative.

That's it: letter, synopsis, sample chapters.

Now all you have to do is make each of them like Elizabeth Taylor in *A Place in the Sun*—irresistible.

The Non-Fiction Proposal

The non-fiction book proposal is a bit more detailed. It has to include a complete outline of the contents and an analysis of the market and competing books. You'll also have to sell yourself as having the expertise and platform to make this a good investment for the publisher.

If you are serious about pursuing a traditional publishing contract for your non-fiction book, the best resource I can recommend is the book *How to Write a Book Proposal* by Michael Larsen (Writer's Digest Books). It covers the entire process with abundant examples.

Even if you eventually decide to self-publish, going through the proposal writing stage will benefit your own efforts, especially with regard to marketing.

For further tips, see the chapter How to Write Non-Fiction For Profit.

12. A Short Course on Self-Publishing

So maybe you've tried the traditional route and couldn't even get inside the Forbidden City.

Or maybe you did get inside but things did not work out as you and your publisher and your agent had hoped. Your books did not sell through. The publisher decides not to offer you another contract.

Should you go look for another publisher? Problem: your sales numbers will be dragging you down like chains on an overboard pirate.

You need to handle your career with eyes wide open, so let me give you the thoughts of Eileen Goudge, a mega-bestselling author from the 1990s whose career stalled in the following decade:

> The cold, hard truth is this: If the sales figures for your last title weren't impressive enough to get booksellers to order your next title in sufficient quantities to make an impact, you're basically screwed. It doesn't matter if your previous titles sold a combined

six million copies worldwide. You're only as good as your last sell-through.

What's even more dispiriting is that you're perceived as a "failure" by publishers when your sales haven't dropped but aren't growing. You become a flat line on a graph. The publisher loses interest and drops the ball, then your sales really do tank. Worse, your poor performance, or "track" as it's known, is like toilet paper stuck to your shoe, following you wherever you go in trying to get a deal with another publisher.

Goudge has new life now as self-publishing author. This, she says, has given her hope and a new burst of creative energy.

Indie publishing is here for you, too.

Or maybe you are jumping into self-publishing from the get-go. That's fine, so long as you remember what I stated earlier, that this is not about getting rich quick and will require, most likely, a period of years to make good money.

But look at it this way: pursuing a traditional career also requires years. Some writers feel their odds of making bank are better if they dedicate those years to self-publishing.

When I started my own self-publishing stream back in 2010, I set out to study and test the best practices. I read all the leading blogs, followed the top authors. I analyzed what was working for me and others and developed what I call The 5 Absolutely Unbreakable Laws of Self-Publishing Success. While there is a sea of resources available to help you with various details on every subject, from formatting to cover design to uploading to marketing, all your activity must be built upon the following five principles.

Law #1 – You Must Think Like a Publisher

Super-successful indie writer Bella Andre said in an interview, "I have an economics background and I've always been entrepreneurial. This is the perfect sweet spot for me, someone who understands how to run a business, really enjoys building a brand and marketing but also has a deep creative strain."

You can find your own sweet spot if you learn to think like a publisher.

There are three main functions of a publishing house: acquisitions, production and marketing. Everything a publisher does falls under one of these umbrellas.

You need to think that way, too.

Acquisitions

In a publishing house there are weekly meetings of what's called a pub board. This is usually made up of representatives from editorial and sales, along with the publisher. At this meeting editors present projects they believe the publisher should buy and bring to market.

The editors have to convince sales that the book is commercial enough that the company can make money from it, and that the author is one who deserves their investment.

The editors are always trying to find a "fresh voice." The sales team is always trying to find commercial viability.

So in thinking like a publisher, and considering your own projects, put those two things together: your voice and what has a chance to sell.

Production

When a book goes into production, there is a series of steps the publishing company has long since followed. You need to do the same (see Law #3, below).

Included in this is a physical print copy of your book. You will want to go through the same quality controls as you prep your print version. I use CreateSpace, Amazon's print-on-demand service, and have been extremely pleased.

Other authors choose to go with a company called LightningSource.

Either way, you need a professional-looking layout and print cover. For this, I highly advise you hire the work out to a professional. But you can begin teaching yourself about the important concepts by looking at the articles on www.thebookdesigner.com.

Marketing

Finally, there is a marketing plan for each book. See Law #4.

And since this is a business, let me say I encourage self-publishing writers to set up their own publishing company as a corporation. It's not hard to do. Consider LegalZoom.com as a starting point.

It's not necessary, of course, because you can operate as a sole proprietor. But as your writing income grows there are some advantages to being incorporated and having royalties flow into the corporate account.

Also, incorporation forces you to think like a business and imposes good discipline on your operation. In some cases it may close a sale. Readers who look at the publisher and see only the author's name may hesitate.

And please avoid cutesy names for your company. I am less inclined to buy a book published by Frisky Snowball Books with a cat's face as the logo.

Each state will have its own requirements and associated fees and costs, so set up a discussion with a CPA to discuss your options, including whether to form a Subchapter S or a Limited Liability corporation. Nolo Press (which started off as a self-publishing operation) offers fantastic books on legal issues for the non-lawyer. One of them is *Incorporate Your Business: A Legal Guide to Forming a Corporation in Your State*. Well worth the cost. I also recommend their *Legal Guide for Starting & Running a Small Business*.

Law #2 – You Must Write the Best Books You Can

This means not just writing, but growing as a writer. As mentioned earlier in this book, make self-study a part of your regular and systematic practices. In the last chapter you'll find a list of titles covering both fiction and non-fiction writing. If you don't know where else to start, start with these.

I also highly recommend that you subscribe to Writer's Digest magazine. This is the premier writer's publication, and each month it's packed with articles on the craft. Read all of them, even if the particular article is not in your field of concentration. The more you know about the writing world, the better.

And when you do read an article that teaches you something about your craft, immediately incorporate that into your current project. Or do a writing exercise that practices the technique.

Do this systematically and you will soon feel yourself growing stronger as a writer. That, in turn, fuels your excitement and motivation.

Law #3 – You Must Prepare Your Book With Quality Controls

As Brian Tracy puts it, "The companies with the highest quality are the companies that earn the highest profits. They represent the greatest opportunities for the future."

Remember, you are in business, and you need a checklist for the essential quality factors for your book production.

For self-publishers, this is the list:

1. Your writing
2. Editing
3. Cover design

4. Marketing copy
5. Formatting
6. Distribution

Some writers just want to write. The idea of learning tech stuff, like formatting an ebook, fills them with dread. I understand that. It would be nice to be Emily Dickinson.

If this is you, let me encourage you to take small bites at learning various technical details. Don't try to gobble it all up at once. I think you'll find it's not the terrible, horrible brain drain you fear.

For example, I use the writing program Scrivener for my books. When I'm finished with the drafts and edits and cover design, a touch of a button produces a digital version of the book ready for upload.

Scrivener takes a bit of time to learn but is well worth it. I recommend the Joseph Michael program Learn Scrivener Fast for this purpose.

In addition to learning on your own, you will need to begin to put together a team for your project. These are professionals who know what they're doing in all of the areas mentioned above. Let's look at each.

Editors

There are three main areas of editing you're going to need:

1. Developmental

2. Copy

3. Proof

The developmental edit is a "big picture" job. It takes in your book as a whole and asks questions about structure, plot and characterization. In the grand old days of publishing, basically most of the twentieth century, publishing houses had star editors in-house who could spend a lot of time working with a writer on the overall manuscript. Maxwell Perkins, for example, was a legendary editor at Scribner's, where he nurtured writers like F. Scott Fitzgerald, Ernest Hemingway, and Thomas Wolfe.

Most publishing houses cannot afford the luxury of an editor like this anymore. That role has been replaced by what is sometimes called a "book doctor."

You can now find abundant book doctors/developmental editors out there doing freelance work. I would also recommend that you check out the Writer's Digest 2d Draft service.

The developmental edit will be the most expensive editing service you'll pay for. But you should consider it an educational investment (not to mention a tax write-off), especially early in your career. A good developmental edit is gold to you.

As you move further along in your writing, you may choose to substitute a team of beta readers for the developmental edit.

The copy editor looks for inconsistencies in content (does your character have blue eyes in Chapter 1, and green eyes in Chapter 30? Unless you're writing paranormal, you don't want that). A good copy editor will also look at the flow of the narrative, helping the author tell the story as effectively as possible. Finally, the copy editor fixes grammar and punctuation problems.

Some publishing professionals break down the process further by adding a "line edit." This is a separate pass looking at the narrative flow, as mentioned above. There can be a bit of confusion here because this level can overlap the copy edit, depending on who is doing the defining. When you work with an editor, talk this over up front to be sure about what you're getting.

Finally, the proofreader cleans up all those nasty typos that seem to infest books (even those produced by big publishing houses) like sand fleas. I've been tortured by them on occasion, despite my best efforts. One advantage to self-publishing is that if a reader notifies you about a typo, you can fix it quickly and easily. I trust if you find one here, you will let me know!

A good proofreader is worth hanging onto. I've always said the proofreaders of the world should untie and from a union. [Note: previous sentence intentional. No words were harmed in the formulation of the joke.]

In this, as in all of your searches for freelancers, live by my axiom: *Caveat scriptor*. Let the writer beware! Re-read the section on "Getting Feedback" in the chapter Secrets of a Winning System for suggestions on finding good freelancers.

Cover Design

In 2008, when self-publishing on Amazon started to take off, quickie books proliferated like rabbits on steroids. Most of these had quickie covers, too, designed by the authors themselves.

They were mostly horrible.

Because cover design is not for amateurs.

Pay for a cover. There are abundant sources out there now for getting a good cover design. Do a little Google searching. Check out a website called 99Designs.com. The basic range for a pro cover is around $200-$500. If you want something more complex and specific, you might pay an artist a bit more. I am not convinced that going into four figures for a book cover is worth it.

There are places that are cheaper or give you design elements to do your own covers. You can select from pre-loaded templates and certain text fonts and the like. I've never seen one of these covers look as good as a pro cover, but you are certainly free to explore this option.

Your cover is super important. It does help you sell books. In fact, the extra money you pay for a great cover will usually be made up in extra sales. Consider it a worthy investment. Here are the steps to go through:

1. Get a recommendation

The best way to find a good cover artist is by recommendation. Your fellow writers with covers you like are the place to start. You can also find artist with our old friend Google. Just be sure to sample their portfolios. If they don't have a portfolio, get out of there fast.

2. Be clear on the process

My preferred method is to be able to suggest a concept and get two preliminary sketches or renderings. Then choose one and have two rounds of modifications and a final polish. Artists may dicker on this, but don't be afraid to dicker right back. If they want a bit more in their price for this, consider it if you really like their work.

3. Give as much specificity as possible

Provide the artist with your genre, the book description (cover copy), and whatever ideas you have about what the cover might look like.

How do you get such ideas? By finding other covers you like and sending links to those images to the artist.

Marketing Copy

This refers primarily to the book description you post for the online retailers. I have devoted Chapter 14 to this.

Formatting

The final step before putting your book out for sale is getting it formatted properly. I've already mentioned Scrivener as an aid to formatting. There is also a program many self-publishers used called Calibre.

You can also find abundant formatting services that will prepare your digital files as well as the layout for your print version.

Again, search and investigate with *caveat scriptor* in mind.

Distribution

Now you're ready to get your book to market. That means uploading to the various retailers you choose to work with. You have two choices:

1. Set up accounts with each retailer and upload the book yourself.

2. Use a "one stop" service to do all that for you.

I recommend #1, because it's not that hard to do, it gives you the greatest flexibility and it doesn't cost you added fees or percentages.

A one-stop service, like BookBaby and Smashwords, will distribute your ebook for a fee or percentage of your royalties. The advantage to the one-stop shop is that you don't have to think about the distribution details. You have one place that uploads your books and collects the dough and pays you.

On the other hand, you lose certain advantages. If, for example, you want to change the price of a book, it can sometimes take weeks to get that to happen. That makes it harder to run an ad on a book-deal service like Bookbub, BookGorilla, BookSends, eBookSoda and so on.

There is a further option to consider: publishing exclusively through Amazon via their Kindle Select program. See my discussion of this option in the next chapter.

I need to mention one other thing here. There are several digital imprints, some offered by big name publishers, that offer you a way to publish your book in return for huge fees. They will try to upsell you marketing services, too, which run into the many thousands of dollars. I cannot recommend this path to you. Spend your dollars on quality editing, cover design and, if need be, formatting. Then publish the book yourself.

Avoid marketing services that cost thousands of dollars. The return is not worth it, in my view. You are better off using the principles below and in the next chapter.

Law #4 – You Must Develop and Work a Marketing Plan

There are mountains of books and blogs and articles and consultants that offer endless advice on marketing strategies. One of the best is Joanna Penn's *How to Market a Book,* which should be in every author's library.

All this information can be confusing. What works best? What should you spend your time on? How can you market and write at the same time? What price should I make my books?

You need to develop a *written* plan and then work it with good ROI—Return on Investment (of money, time and energy). As someone who's been studying marketing for well over two decades, I will try to cut through the noise for you in the next chapter.

A Note on Pricing

Choosing the right price for your book is a matter of strategy first and ultimate revenue second.

In the beginning, your strategy is to get as many eyeballs on your work as possible. This means you might consider the "free" option via Amazon's Select Program.

You could also opt for 99¢ across multiple channels.

For full length novels, there have been surveys that show the "sweet spot" to be $2.99-$4.99.

If you have a series of three or more books, many authors, including this one, have had great success making the first book in the series "perma-free." Since Amazon does not (as of this writing) allow books to be priced free at first, have the book published on Kobo, which does allow the free pricing option. You can also get your book listed free on Barnes & Noble, though the process involves using an aggregator like Smashwords to do it. You then go to your book's page on Amazon and scroll down to just below the ranking. There you'll see a link to report a lower price:

Amazon Best Sellers Rank: #97 Paid in Kindle Store (See Top 100 Paid in Kindle Store)
#3 in Kindle Store > Kindle eBooks > Mystery, Thriller & Suspense > **Crime Fiction**
#5 in Kindle Store > Kindle eBooks > Mystery, Thriller & Suspense > Thrillers > **Crime**
#8 in Books > Mystery, Thriller & Suspense > Thrillers & Suspense > **Crime**

Would you like to **give feedback on images** or **tell us about a lower price**?

You'll then be asked for the URL for the lower price site.

I was able to make *City of Angels,* Book 1 in my Trials of Kit Shannon series, perma-free simply by going free at Kobo then reporting the lower price myself. Other writers report they've had to ask friends to help them out by also reporting the lower price.

If all else fails, email Amazon customer support and they should take care of it for you.

When *City of Angels* went perma-free, downloads skyrocketed. Without my knowledge or effort, it was picked up by blogs and sites that report on free Kindle deals. The other books in the series saw an uptick in sales.

Don't be afraid to experiment. When I make price changes I usually do so at the end of a month, so it's easy for me to track data and compare it to other months. This is one reason I have direct accounts with retailers. It's much easier to play around.

Law #5 – You Must Repeat Over and Over For the Rest of Your Life

Self-publishing is a volume business. The more quality (key word!) work you put out there, the better your chances of an increasing income stream.

How good are the chances?

Better than if you put all your hopes on one or two books. Don't fall into that trap. You will likely feel disappointed the first few turns around the track, because you've heard stories like this:

Bella Andre was a traditionally-published category romance writer in 2010. She'd done eight books for two different publishers without much financial success.

Self-publishing was just coming into its own, and at a friend's suggestion Andre decided to give it a try.

She uploaded her first ebook, *Love Me*, and priced it at $3.99. In one month she made $20,000, which was four times as much as any book contract she ever signed. She put up another ebook a few months later and it became the first self-published title to hit Amazon's top-25 best sellers list.

Andre was in the right place at the right time with the right product (romance) and the right work ethic. Between 2010 and 2014, Andre put out thirty—count 'em, thirty—ebooks. Her earnings over that time? All she will say is that it is in the "eight figures."

This is not a peak many writers will ever reach.

That should not discourage you. Because in the strata under people like Bella Andre and Hugh Howey are a large and increasing number of authors who are making very good money as writers.

Some of these choose to quit their day jobs.

Some are making enough for car payments or mortgages or the kids' educations.

And the great part about being a self-publishing writer is that no one can stop you.

You get to keep going. You get to keep trying. You get to keep getting better. You don't have to sit down with someone telling you you're not capable, that you should just quit, that you should go away and leave your dreams to others. You don't have to take that as long as you've got a keyboard and an imagination.

And in this way, you can never be defeated.

A Few More Business Principles for Self-Publishers

• *Don't be afraid to pay a little extra for quality*

This is especially true when it comes to book covers, formatting text for digital and print, and editing. The old "you get what you pay for" rule applies across the board.

Obviously you should stay within a normal range. You can easily find out what that is with a bit of googling. But let's say you have the choice between two cover artists. One charges $500 for a cover, but her work is awesome and right for your genre. Another charges $350 and is pretty good. Go ahead and spend the extra yard and a half.

• *Get stuff in writing before you pay*

For any work you pay for, be sure the terms are clear to you and are in writing. An email is fine so long as both parties are agreed upon what's expected.

• *Buy a set of ISBN numbers*

You will need an ISBN for the print edition of your books. This is the book identifier number used by multiple outlets, including bookstores and libraries, to keep track of print books. It is not required for digital editions. If you publish your print version via CreateSpace (Amazon's program), you can have them assign you a number, but then CreateSpace will be listed as the publisher.

If you want your publishing company listed, you need your own ISBNs. Purchasing them one at a time is expensive. But you can save by buying them in lots directly from Bowker, the official ISBN company. Do not purchase ISBNs from any other service.

Bowker's site is MyIdentifiers.com.

• *Do I need to register my copyright?*

Copyright law is complex. What you need to know is this: you own the copyright for the works you create without registering them with the U.S. Copyright office. What registration does is offer you greater legal leverage should you ever feel a need to sue someone for infringement—but only in the United States. Other countries have their own ways of handling copyright matters.

So do you *need* to register the copyright? No. Should you? That depends on if you desire extra protection and don't mind instituting legal proceedings (which runs into money). The registration process is easy and not that expensive. Go to the U.S. Copyright office page for more.

• *Respect but don't obsess over data*

There is a fine line between knowing the stats your self-publishing generates and living your life around them. Some authors check their Amazon rank several times a day. That can only lead to madness and walking the streets talking to yourself.

Be systematic about it. My own practice is this:

Once a month I analyze my latest Amazon sales report. I can do this via the downloaded spreadsheet and the Kindle dashboard. The latter is a convenient way to look at the sales of specific titles. I am looking at sales trends and price comparisons. Lower performing titles will become the subject of "goosing," explained below.

If I'm running a special promotion or have a deal-service ad, I'll track sales by the day for awhile.

What I don't want to do is take too much mental energy away from the most important thing I do—write.

• *Think series potential*

Write a killer book with an irresistible protagonist...and think in terms of series. Series have the potential to grow an extensive readership like nothing else.

Lee Child's Jack Reacher is an example from the traditional publishing world.

James Bond from the past.

Numerous self-publishing authors are doing quite well with a series character. And many are finding that after three or four books, making the first in the series perma-free is money.

• *Think foreign*

The opening up of foreign markets for self-publishers is only going to get better. Once you're established on Amazon here at home, consider spreading into other countries. Check out the following sites: PubMatch.com and iprelicense.com. These services work to match your books with foreign markets,. You can make a deal similar to what ACX does for audio books (see my chapter on adding audio-books to your repertoire), which means you don't have to spend a huge amount of money up front.

• *Use bitly links*

Bitly.com is a way for you to keep track of click-throughs on links you provide for your books. It's a great way to measure the success of certain promotions.

You should also use a bitly link in the back of your ebooks when they go to an Amazon ordering page. That's because some devices with an "i" in front of the name won't let the owners go to Amazon via a direct link. If someone is reading on such a device and they reach the end of your book and see that the next in the series is offered, a direct Amazon link won't get them there. They'll have to do extra work. A bitly link works around that.

• *Goosing a stalled title*

There are several ways you can give an older title a little push upward. Here are a few:

- A deal-alert ad. This is where you drop the price for a time and pay for placement with a BookBub or a BookGorilla-type of service.

- Drop the price and promote through social media. Remember, though, that you must build up trust on social media before you hawk anything. And when you do, don't overkill. See it as a way to tell your followers about a deal they can take advantage of. You're offering them value.

- Change the cover. This is a bit pricey, but if you do it right it's an investment that should pay off with increased sales. See the cover design discussion, above.

- Write a guest blog post on a subject relating to your book. If your novel is a political thriller, write about your research. If it's a romance, write about why you chose an Alpha male instead of a Beta male. Whatever. Pitch your idea to popular blogs that cover your genre.

- Cross-promote with other writing friends. Talk each other up on social media. When you are recommended by someone else that's better than tooting your own horn.

The Future of Self-Publishing

The only thing certain about the future of publishing in general, and self-publishing in particular, is that it is uncertain. Change is the new normal.

Which makes for an exciting and adventurous journey. When fellow pro writers have expressed their dismay and anxiety to me (e.g., about whether they need to go indie or stick it out with a publisher) I tell them to be a cork. Change and disruption are the roiling sea. Writers need to be floating on the surface, sensing the currents, and exploiting their options.

Big honking changes may occur. What is big now may be small later, or even disappear.

Writers will never disappear.

We do know this. Never again will there be only one way to publish and reach readers. I find that the best news of all.

So there it is. My short course on self-publishing. I've tried to give you the most important things to think about and establish. Follow the advice in this chapter and you can build upon it.

Continue to devote some time each week, half-an-hour to an hour, to the study of self-publishing. Find the best blogs to follow. Here are a few you can start with:

Thecreativepenn.com
Thepassivevoice.com
HughHowey.com
DavidGaughran.wordpress.com

If you study the business right alongside your study of the writing craft, and keep up your creativity time as well, you know what? You'll not only have a full writing life, you won't have all that much time to be *anxious* about your writing life.

That's a very good place to be.

13. What You Need to Know About Marketing

There's an old saying in sales: We know that 20% of marketing works; we just don't know which 20%.

That's a bit tongue-in-cheek, but perhaps not the whole tongue. With so many marketing options available, it's hard to test what works. Further, what works for one book may not work the same way for the next.

As a result, many authors spend way too much time stressing about marketing and throwing everything they can think of at the wall, hoping some of it will stick.

Quite often this results in loss of sleep and quality writing time (the latter being your most important asset).

So here are the 10 most important things you need to know about marketing. Concentrate on these and the marketing side of your career will go a lot more smoothly than if you try to do everything at once.

1. The best marketing is your writing

All the pizzazz in the world won't sell bad writing. You can use dazzle to get an introduction. You can spend a lot of money to get readers to give your book a try. But from that point on, the writing does all the heavy lifting.

As one of the bestselling authors of all time, Mickey Spillane, once put it, "Your first chapter sells your book. Your last chapter sells your next book."

To me, that's good news. I don't need to stress about all the marketing options out there. I know that the most important thing I can do is produce books worth reading.

Back in 2011, Smashwords did a survey of readers on how they selected ebooks:

1. Word of Mouth: 51%

   a. From reader recommends on forums, blogs, online message boards: 29%

   b. Looking for their favorite authors: 18%

   c. Personal friend/family member recommends: 4%

2. Browse randomly online, then check the reviews: 7%

3. "Also bought" recommendation from online retailer: 5%

4. Read a free ebook, then buy others by author if I like it: 5%

5. Bestseller lists in favorite genres: 3%

No magic here, not gaming the system. Write the best book you can every time out. Get people talking about your work.

2. Follow the 80/20 rule

There are innumerable options for taking your books to market. So what do you select?

The 80/20 rule helps. Sometimes called the Pareto Principle (named for the Italian economist who formulated it) the rule holds that 80% of your results will come from 20% of your efforts. Your job is to find the top 20% and concentrate on them.

The rest of this list is my view of what that 20% is.

3. Create an easy-to-navigate website

To me, a fancy, graphics-heavy author website is a burden (especially if it has sound!) What I want is a site that is easy to navigate gives me the information I want, fast.

Most consumers want that, too. They don't want to waste time for animation to load. They don't want to have to mute the music.

So give them a clean home page that features your latest book.

Have an "About the Author" page, where you can shine. Have a professionally taken author photo for this page.

Give each book its own page, with cover and description, blurbs and reviews, and links to retail sites.

Have a page for news and appearances.

List your social media sites.

Most important, make it easy for people to sign up for your email list. Assure them that their email addresses will never be given out to anyone for any reason.

4. The best way to market is by going out to your own list of readers

The saddest writing career these days is that of the so-called midlist writer. That refers to an author with a major publisher who is not in the bestselling ranks. Therefore he is consigned to the back pages of a catalogue and if things don't turn around quickly will likely be dropped by the house.

The much better position now is what I call the ownlist writer. It's the writer who owns his own list of fans. This is where the gold is. This is what you need to grow.

There's a concept out there called 1000 True Fans. It holds that you don't need a monster list of people in order to gain momentum for your books. If you can get to one thousand dedicated fans, you will have a guaranteed way to sell your new offerings.

My email list is my most valuable marketing tool. It keeps growing and delivering results. Here are the principles I use:

Text, not newsletter

I want my email to look like an email, as if coming from a friend. Because that's what my readers are to me. I don't want my email to look like a fancy newsletter or promotional brochure. While I don't have any data to compare which format works better (I could run tests myself, but don't feel like it), I do have anecdotal evidence from my readers that confirm my choice.

Brief

I don't write long emails. I understand people are pressed for time.

Once a month on average

I try to keep in touch with my list an average of once a month. More than that would get annoying. Less than that can begin to lose touch. It's not exact. There have been times I've skipped a month because I really didn't have anything new to add. But this is my goal.

Content that is relevant and pleasing

My emails usually have three things: something personal about my writing life, a link to a new deal or a reminder about an existing one, and something amusing that makes the email fun to read. Recently I received a response to one my updates, in which the sender said, "I was introduced to you by email (you were kind enough to write me when I emailed you my delight in your first book)...so I wanted to continue the "tradition" of letting you know I enjoy not only your books and fabulous writing style, but the updates and humorous insights via your emails!"

That's the way it's supposed to work.

Scott Smith, a king of email list building, concurs. One of his pillars for successful emails is "show your personality." In *Email Marketing Blueprint* he writes:

> Competition is fierce in every market. Subscribers aren't afraid to leave a list because they know it's easy to find 30 more. Really, the only way to stand out is to showcase a genuine, helpful personality.
>
> Maintain a friendly tone in your emails — like you're having a one on one conversation with a buddy.

Start your list building by opening an account with an email service like MailChimp, ConstantContact or VerticalResponse. Put links to your home page in the back matter of your books and invite readers to sign up. I do a monthly giveaway for new sign-ups, with the offer of a free book as a prize.

The best way to study what works is to see how others are doing it. If you'd like to see my methods in action, all you have to do is sign up at my website: www.jamesscottbell.com.

5. Deal-alert services are worth the money

Many services exist to inform readers of digital book deals. You sign up to receive their emails and tell them what genres you like. They send you an email each day with an offering of ebooks in your preferred genres at discounted prices.

BookBub, as I write, is the biggest. It curates its submissions so it can be hard to get included at first. They like well-reviewed books with a certain market presence. Go to their website and look at their tips. Keep trying.

Other good services include BookSends, BookGorilla, Kindle Nation Daily, eBookSoda, Ereader News Today. There will be more coming along.

Now here's the most important thing. Some authors don't break even (that is, make back in sales the amount they paid for placement) and therefore conclude it's not worth the investment.

Wrong.

What you need are readers, and paying to get them should be part of your long-term strategy. Even if you don't break even on a placement initially, the odds are you will over time. Because some of those new readers will become your fans and purchase your next book without your having to buy their attention.

So the value of a new reader is greater than just the initial sale.

Plan to use these services for all your books on a rotating basis. Map out placement strategies month by month, for one year in advance. Some authors even

hire "virtual assistants" to do the work of filling out
the forms on a regular basis.

6. Use social media for building trust

When Facebook and Twitter began to explode,
businesses hopped on board in a big way, thinking
that this was marketing Valhalla. Millions and millions
of eyeballs would see their marketing posts and
tweets, and selling stuff would be easy-peasy.

Oops.

Write this down on your brain: Social media is not
a good way to sell books.

This will save you a lot of time and keep you from
alienating scores of potential readers.

We now know that FB and Twitter are not good
for direct marketing. They are actually *social* media.
Imagine that. People are there for relationships and
not to be spammed.

Early on I followed some authors on Twitter who
simply used "buy my book" type tweets several times
a day, every day.

Their books never went anywhere, and they did
not appear to have quality followers.

Use social media to build trust with followers.
You do that by offering them information that makes
their life more enjoyable. You actually engage and
respond and, in short, make yourself a welcome guest.

Then, when it does come time to announce a
book or a deal, you have earned the right to do so.
Your followers will, in turn, spread the word for you.

Use the 80/20 rule here, too. Don't overspend
your time on social media. I advocate picking one or

two venues and specializing. My preferred choice is Twitter. I'm @jamesscottbell.

7. Amazon programs

As of this writing, the Select program from Amazon's Kindle Digital Publishing is a good option when you're just starting out. You publish your book exclusively with Amazon for a minimum of ninety days, and during that time you can list your book for free for five days. Choose five days in a row and get the word out. Ask your fans and family to spread the glad tidings.

Some well-established authors extol the virtues of Amazon exclusivity. Others advocate getting your book out to as many channels as possible. The calculus on which route is better seems to change from month to month. That's because other retailers, such as Barnes & Noble, Kobo and Apple fluctuate in their market presence.

Some authors choose a path based on principle, even if it might cost them some revenue. This is a question only you can answer, so do some research on the virtues of each. Examine the arguments and decide which feels right for you. You can always change your mind later and switch tactics.

Amazon has also begun a subscription service called Kindle Unlimited. For a monthly fee, readers have unlimited access to Kindle books (though at the moment the major publishers have not opted in). If you are in the Select program your book will be part of the KU library. Payment comes from a KU fund and how much it will be per book is not entirely clear.

There has been a lot of talk and uncertainty about KU and what it means for authors. Some Googling will get you a ton of information. While it's too early right now to render any certainty, always keep an eye on what Amazon is doing for independent authors. It is still the largest bookseller in the world.

Hugh Howey, one of the mega-stars of self-publishing, has come down (at least at the time of this writing) on the side of exclusivity:

> As the time ticks down on my trial run in KU, which way am I leaning? Toward exclusivity. A larger readership is only one advantage. It'll also be easier to keep my works up to date by only having to upload to a single site. Another bonus will be to concentrate my sales into a single set of bestseller lists. One of the drawbacks of being published everywhere is the reduction of visibility, ironically. The more sales are concentrated in a single outlet, the higher your ebooks will be on bestseller lists, and the more prominent to casual browsers. Reviews will also be more concentrated. Like with the publishing house analogy earlier, all efforts are channeled into the biggest sales outlet.

Finally, Amazon offers all its authors their own author page via Author Central. Keep this page updated and relevant. Look at the pages of bestselling authors and emulate what looks good. Remember, you can learn whatever you need to know.

8. The blogging issue

When blogs (do you recall that the term is short for weblog?) first took off, they were mainly there for people to share about their lives and interests so friends and family and maybe a few interested others could follow along.

Of course, people soon began to see them as ways to make money, and many did. Some by creating popular blogs and turning that content into books. Others by gaining large followings and selling directly.

Times have changed, and two forces conspire against successful blogging: 1) there are innumerable blogs out there now; and 2) people have less time in their busy lives to devote to reading them.

We must, however, recognize a difference between fiction writers trying to use a blog for "platforming," and non-fiction writers devoted to a subject matter.

Blogging is a huge time suck for fiction writers. And then there's the challenge of content: How are you going to come up with fresh material three times a week? That energy would probably be better spent following Rule #1, above.

Still, some novelists like blogging, no matter their traffic. If that's you, then use your blog as another way to communicate with loyal fans. Make it about community, and building trust and good will. Count the cost of the ROI and if you still want to commit, go for it.

Many non-fiction writers have one area of interest or expertise, and that becomes the focus of their blogging. This can work out nicely, for then the blog posts can be gathered and woven into books. I've done this with the weekly posts I write for the blog Kill Zone. So far I have self-published two how-to-write collections, and will likely do more.

Note, my blogging is not a pain because I love the subject—the craft of writing and the writing life—and once-a-week does not over-tax my time.

If "blogging a book" seems like a good idea to you, let me recommend Nina Amir's *How to Blog a Book* (Writer's Digest Books). The title says it all.

Is there an alternative to blogging?

There is.

Build relationships with four or five highly-trafficked blogs. These blogs should be related to the subject matter and genre of your books. You build relationships by leaving quality comments on posts and not being a boor. When you're ready to launch your book approach the blog administrator about doing a guest post. Some will say yes. Some will say another time. Some will say no. Drop the latter from your blog list and find replacements. See #10, below.

9. Blog tours

You can pay money for a company to set up a blog tour. For a fee, you get to post content on blogs that cater to the kind of readers you're looking for.

Blog tours are not as effective as the other things mentioned in this chapter. Still, it's one way to get eyeballs on your books if you're just starting out. But keep your expectations low and do your due diligence in researching services. If you can get recommendations from satisfied authors, so much the better.

And how do you get such recommendations? This way—

10. Network with other writers

The writing community is, by and large, generous and supportive. You find like-minded scribes via the internet (on places like KindleBoards) and live conferences. I'm a big advocate of going to quality writing conferences as a way to learn and meet other authors.

If you specialize in a genre, there are conferences that will cater to your interests. For example, mystery and suspense writers love Bouchercon. The authors who gather (usually starting around 5 p.m., in the bar) are convivial and supportive. It's good to have that vibe from time to time. Writing is lonely enough.

You should also get involved with online writers groups and forums, and join in the many discussions happening in social media. Angela Ackerman says, "Facebook and Twitter are huge for writers groups and networking, and following writer-centric blogs is also a great way to start conversations that can become tight friendships."

So there you have it, my personal list of the best ways to market your books. Do your own research and add to or modify this list as you see fit. Just remember these last two rules:

- Do something to market your books

- But don't do so much that your writing suffers

14. Book Descriptions That Sell

Book descriptions (sometimes called cover copy) are what you use to entice browsing readers to take a chance on your book. Every time a reader plunks down money on a book, she's taking a risk. This is true even if the author is a known quantity. Not every book is a home run.

So each time out you must convince that reader to part with discretionary cash.

The key to understanding this kind of copy is that it is *sequential*. What you need to do is grab with a headline and move browsers along to the point where they will want to sample or purchase your book.

Every part of the copy must nudge the reader to the next part.

Start With Your Elevator Pitch

Every book you write needs an elevator pitch.

Every single one. It will help you focus your material and determine your book's marketability. Without it, you're throwing spaghetti at the wall hoping some of it sticks.

What is an elevator pitch? It's what you can say to an interested party in the time it takes to ride an elevator several floors. People are inundated with sales messages every day. You've got to stand out in all that clutter and do so in thirty seconds.

So let's say you get on an elevator in Beverly Hills and Steven Spielberg hops in. He nods and smiles and sees your baseball cap with *Writer* on it. As the doors close he asks what you've written.

You say, "Um, a book. It's kind of an idea that came to me when I was visiting my grandmother in Iowa. I don't normally go to Iowa, so I wasn't really thinking about writing a book about it, but when I got there, when I got off the plane, the whole place just smelled different. I live here in L.A., so you get what I'm saying. Anyway ... my grandmother was taken to the hospital, I found out, because her urine was pink. So I rushed out to ..."

Ding! The elevator has stopped, the doors open, and Mr. Spielberg gets off without another word.

Opportunity lost.

That's not how you do an elevator pitch.

This is how.

Fiction

Your elevator pitch will consist of three sentences:

Sentence #1 is made up of: Character Name + Vocation + Initial Situation

Example (this comes from a novel called *The Insider*. My thanks to author Reece Hirsch for permission):

> Will Connelly is an associate at a prestigious San Francisco law firm, handling high level merger negotiations between computer companies.

Sentence #2: "When" + Doorway of No Return

The Doorway of No Return is a concept I explain in *Plot & Structure*. Other teachers call it Plot Point I, or the First Act Break. It occurs no later than 1/5 of the way through your novel. It's the event that thrusts your lead character into the conflict of Act II. I call it the Doorway of No Return because once through that door the lead character cannot go back to his ordinary world. He has to face the dangers ahead.

> When Will celebrates by picking up a Russian woman at a club, he finds himself at the mercy of a ring of small-time Russian mobsters with designs on the top-secret NSA computer chip Will's client is developing.

Sentence #3: "Now" + Death Overhanging

The stakes in a novel must be death.

That's right.

Death.

Because anything less than that does not have sufficient stakes for the readers to care to the utmost.

Now, there are three kinds of death: physical, professional, psychological.

A thriller almost always is about physical death. The bad guys want to kill the good guy. An ordinary person stumbles into a dark scheme and gets a target on her back. Without physical death, the thrills are hard to come by.

But there is also professional death. This is where the main plot centers on what the Lead does for a living. A lawyer, a cop, a firefighter, a mother. There isn't necessarily a villain seeking the death of the Lead. So what you, the writer, need to do is make the plot a matter of this person's very livelihood or role. If the Lead fails, their career is effectively over. (For example, the lawyer's last chance at redemption in *The Verdict*, a novel by Barry Reed and the movie starring Paul Newman).

Justify the professional death aspect by building up the extreme importance of the vocation to the Lead.

Then there is psychological death. This is where the character has to deal with an emotional, spiritual or otherwise internal crisis. If she doesn't resolve it, her physical life will go on but she will have "died on the inside." Examples of such books (usually literary or character-driven novels) are The Cather in the Rye by J. D. Salinger and White Oleander by Janet Fitch.

Our example is a thriller, so physical death is on the line:

Now, with the Russian mob, the SEC and the Department of Justice all after him, Will has to find a way to save his professional life and his own skin before the wrong people get the technology for mass destruction.

And there you have it. The perfect elevator pitch. You are free to play with the wording, but this formula will give you all you need for that convincing sales talk on a short elevator ride.

Here are a few other examples:

The Wizard of Oz

Dorothy Gale is a farm girl who dreams of getting out of Kansas to a land far, far away, where she and her dog will be safe from the likes of town busybody Miss Gulch.

When a twister hits the farm, Dorothy is transported to a land of strange creatures and at least one wicked witch who wants to kill her.

Now, with the help of three unlikely friends, Dorothy must find a way to destroy the wicked witch so the great

wizard will send her back
home.

Star Wars

Luke Skywalker is a farm boy
on an obscure planet who
dreams of becoming a Jedi
knight.

When the forces of the
Empire murder his aunt and
uncle, Luke takes off to join
the rebellion.

Now he must learn the ways
of the Force so he can fight
the legions led by Darth
Vader, the evil overlord bent
on destroying the rebels.

Non-Fiction

For non-fiction we'll use three paragraphs, or
blocks, for our pitch.

Paragraph #1: The Most Gripping Question +
The Specific Answer

What does every man secretly
desire? The ability to kick any
other man's butt.

Paragraph #2: In [Title] You'll Learn + Bullet Point Benefits

In *How to Kick Any Man's Butt* you'll learn...

- the key to victory in any street fighting situation
- the 7 best take down moves
- the Chuck Norris secret for ultimate confidence

Paragraph #3: About the Author (why should we trust you?)

Joe Doakes was a bouncer and bartender in New York's Hell's Kitchen before joining the Navy SEALs. He has been teaching street fighting for over 20 years. His list of clients includes Brad Pitt, Richard Simmons and Barak Obama.

The Book Description

You've got your elevator pitch. All you have to do now is add two things: a headline and (for fiction) an About the Author squib. If you have received a blurb from a well-known author or, in the case of non-fiction, an expert in the field, you can add that as well.

Headline

Think of your headline as the hook, the grabber, the tease. A good headline is short, intriguing, and captures the essence of the book.

Not something you just dash off. You need a method. And I'm here to give it to you.

Fiction:

For a novel or story, you need an adjective, noun, and verb.

Let's start with the *noun*.

That is what your character is, her job or vocation. What does your character do? Is she a lawyer, doctor, cop, mother, model?

Name it.

Next, add an adjective/phrase that describes her a little more fully. What *kind* of lawyer, doctor, cop, mother, etc.?

Insecure cop
Criminal lawyer
Overworked mother
Aging model

Finally, the verb phrase, which talks about the main action of the main plot.

For my novelette about a vigilante nun who uses street fighting to battle the criminal element (*Force of Habit*) I came up with the following:

A vigilante nun cleans up the streets of Los Angeles. Sinners beware.

Non-Fiction:

You can use the question-type headline you already developed. Or you can come up with another take by setting forth the one primary takeaway value for that book.

You can use the "How to" headline (if your book isn't titled that way):

How to feed a family of seventeen on $400 or less a month

How to drive a golf ball over 250 yards every time

How to negotiate anything in ten easy steps

Or something with keys, secrets, techniques, and so on:

The keys to staying fit and trim for the rest of your life

Learn the communications secrets of the greatest conversationalists of all time

A strong statement:

Financial collapse is just around the corner

It's the best time on earth to be a writer

Of course, not all non-fiction is "how to." There are biographies, philosophical and spiritual tomes, memoirs, investigative reporting, essays.

You can find a headline for each if you just give it some thought and remember your target audience.

For a biography of legendary golfer Sam Snead, you would keep golf fans in mind:

He had the sweetest swing of all time. And he was feared.

If epistemology is your thing:

How do you know what you know?

Investigative:

The newspapers buried this story. Now it returns from the grave.

Have fun with this. Brainstorm. Try things out. Write several headlines in rapid succession and tweak the best ones. Ask several friends which one they like best.

The Copy

The all-important book description, or "back cover copy," is your ticket to sales. It's crucially important.

If it looks sloppy or unprofessional, you'll lose sales.

If it doesn't get to the "sizzle" right away, you'll lose sales.

Fortunately, there's a way to make it just right. Your elevator pitch! You've done all the hard work on that, now you can use it to sell your book. You can use it as is or as a starting point.

Let's take a look at examples from both fiction and non-fiction.

Fiction:

For *Force of Habit*, since my main character is summed up in the headline, I dove right into the storyline. I added a blurb I've received and finished off with a little embellishment.

> When a nun is viciously attacked, Sister Justicia takes it upon herself to find out what happened. The cops don't like that. Neither does her Mother Superior at St. Cecelia's. But when a couple of hoods try to stick up a liquor store and Sister J brings them down, something is unleashed inside her . . . something that will either confirm her calling . . . or destroy it.
>
> From "one of the best writers out there, bar none" (Library Review) comes the start of a new series featuring a heroine unlike any other in crime fiction—Sister Justicia Marie, rogue nun.
>
> If criminals are the knuckles, she is the ruler. So be good.

I also write paranormal fiction under the pen name K. Bennett. For my series of zombie legal thrillers with Kensington, the copywriter was top notch. He captured the tone of the books superbly. For book #3 in the series, *I Ate the Sheriff,* here is the headline:

Justice. It's what's for dinner.

And the copy:

> What's worse than killing a cop? Eating him afterwards. Which exactly what happened to a Los Angeles County sheriff on Mulholland Drive. Now Mallory Caine, zombie at law, faces the toughest trial of her life – her own – since she's the prime suspect. Ironically, Mallory's been suppressing her undead desires in a 12-step zombie recovery group. It's her human desires that scare her. He's one hot werewolf named Steve Ravener, and he's Mallory's latest client. His ex-wife wants to keep his kids away from him, and if he hopes to see them again, he needs a lawyer whose bite is worse than his bark. Needless to say, family law has never been this hairy. And with a murder charge hanging over her head, a snake goddess charming her mother, and all kinds of hell-spawn taking

over L.A., Mallory's plate is full. And she's dying to take a bite.

Non-Fiction:

The key to doing non-fiction copy is to stress the benefits and Unique Selling Proposition (USP). Again, your elevator pitch is the copy you'll use.

Here is an example from a book published by McGraw-Hill titled, *How to Talk to Anyone: 92 Little Tricks for Big Success in Relationships.*

Notice how the sub-title itself is a selling phrase, too.

Here are the headline and benefits copy of the aforementioned book:

Become a master communicator and succeed in life, love, and business

Have you ever admired those successful people who seem to have it all? You see them chatting confidently at parties and being listened to in business meetings. They're the ones with the best jobs, nicest parties, and most interesting friends.

But wait a minute. They're not necessarily smarter than you or even better looking. What it comes down to is their more skillful way of communicating with other people. Now How to Talk to Anyone reveals the secrets of successful communication. With Leil Lowndes's ninety-two easy and effective techniques, you will discover how to become a master communicator in life, love, and business.

Combining the latest research with Leil's trademark wit and warm-hearted observations of human foibles, *How to Talk to Anyone* shows you how to:

- Make an unforgettable entrance and meet the people you want to meet
- Sound like an insider in any crowd, no matter how little you have in common
- Use body language to captivate audiences of all sizes
- Work a party the way a politician works a room
- Always come across confident, credible, and charismatic wherever you are

How to Talk to Anyone, which is an update of her popular book, Talking the Winner's Way (see the 5-star reviews of the latter) is based on solid research about techniques that work!

Notice the use of bullet points to get across the benefits. It makes the copy easy to read and accomplishes the sequential strategy we discussed earlier.

Take your time with the headline and the copy. Give it several iterations and get feedback from people. And note that it doesn't have to be long. People have shorter attention spans these days and you want to do what the old-time advertising guys used to say: *Sell the sizzle, not the steak.*

Your copy is the sizzle. The first taste of steak is going to be the sample that's downloaded. That's where you close the sale.

Your book description will also include an "About the Author" section. What do you put in there when you're just starting out?

Whatever is relevant.

And don't be cute about it. Unless you are writing humor (and there's nothing harder than writing humor) don't yuk it up. If you've written a thriller, don't say things like this: *Joe Doakes has been called the "next Harlan Coben" by his Uncle Ralph, who reads a lot of thrillers.*

Readers hate that. They're going to think you're out to scam them.

Just put in material relating to the book, and leave it at that. If you're a lawyer and you've written your first legal thriller, then: *Joe Doakes has been a practicing lawyer in San Francisco for the past twelve years.*

When you start to gather more credits as a writer, or join writers' organizations of note, you can include those: *Joe Doakes is the author of three previous novels in the Geraldo the Avenger series. He is a member of International Thriller Writers and Mystery Writers of America.*

Metadata

Metadata are words and phrases that operate as search engine magnets. If someone goes to Amazon, for example, and types in the search term "courtroom thrillers," results come back for legal thrillers of a variety of types.

In fact, when I typed that in just now here were the top three titles:

Irreparable Harm (Sasha McCandless Legal Thriller Book 1)

Presumption of Innocence (David Brunelle Legal Thriller Book 1)

Proof of Intent: A Charley Sloan Courtroom Thriller

What do you notice about each of the titles? Yep. They have metadata right there in the title line (e.g., *legal thriller, courtroom thriller*).

That's one place for it. But not all authors like to do that.

Another place is to drop keywords into the book description itself, in a way that is unobtrusive. *In this stunning courtroom thriller, the corruption of the system is laid bare.*

You'll also be able to input keywords when you upload your books to publishing platforms.

How do you find the right keywords? You brainstorm, research, and play around. A good place to start is with Google Adwords. Create a free account at adwords.google.com, then go to Tools >> Keyword Planner. Google this: "Keyword planning tool tutorial" and you'll get some instruction on how to use this resource.

For some great tips on using keywords, see the post by Joanna Penn titled, "The Importance Of Keywords For MetaData And The Discoverability Of Your Book."

http://www.thecreativepenn.com/2013/02/28/keywords-metadata-discoverability

15. The Foundations of Successful Fiction

If you're going to write book-length fiction you have to know your craft. That's why I advocate all fiction writers to weekly a) write their quota of words; and b) systematically study the techniques of successful fiction.

The techniques can be learned.

First, what is the big picture? What, after all, is a book-length fictional narrative about?

In simplest terms, a story is the record of how a character, through strength of will, meets the ultimate challenge — facing death.

As I stressed earlier when discussing book descriptions, a novel must be about physical, professional, or psychological death. At least one of those has to be on the line for the stakes to be high enough for readers to care to the max.

Now, in meeting the challenge, the character is going to have to transform in one of two ways: either she will change in a significant way, becoming essentially a different (improved) person, or she will become stronger while remaining essentially the same.

158

Let's look at an example of each.

Scarlett O'Hara transforms into a new and better person at the end of *Gone with the Wind*. She finally realizes her dreams of Ashley and the Old South were never reality and have to be abandoned. She realizes how selfish she's been and that she truly loves Rhett. Unfortunately, it comes too late. Rhett leaves her. But Scarlett determines she will think about how to get Rhett back, tomorrow.

Katniss Everdeen, on the other hand, does not become a new person at the end of The Hunger Games. She is fundamentally the same. But she has grown stronger. She had to in order to survive. Physical death was on the line.

Now that we're clear on the broad overview of story, we turn now to the basics of solid structure: The LOCK System and the three acts. Ignore these at your peril, for without them your books will not sell.

The LOCK System

Back when I was learning the craft, I wanted to see if I could simplify the basics of what makes up a solid novel, every time. My inquiry led me to come up with what I call The LOCK System. This became the basis of an article for *Writer's Digest* magazine that proved to be quite popular. Later it was the foundation for my book *Plot & Structure*. I've taught the system to countless writers over the last fifteen years and seen the positive results.

If you want to write fiction for a living, if you want your books to reach a wide audience, they must have the following:

L is for Lead

Imagine a guy on a New York City corner with a "Will Work for Food" sign. Interesting? Not very. We've seen it many times before, and we wouldn't stand and watch him for two minutes.

This is a clue about your lead character. She has to be interesting. A good story needs a character readers want to follow.

Many writers spend a great deal of time on character biography. How extensively is a matter of taste. At the very least I like to know the following about my lead character: What is her passion in life? What is one major turning point from her childhood? Does she act first and analyze later, or vice versa? What makes this character unique? Why do I love this character?

After conceiving an interesting lead character, you must go a step further and figure out how to create an emotional bond with the reader. You can accomplish this by mastering four dynamics—identification, sympathy, likability and inner conflict.

Identification means the lead is like us. She's not perfect. She has normal human flaws. Your key question here is: What does she do that makes her just like most people? Find those qualities, and readers will begin to warm to the lead.

In *The Girl Who Loved Tom Gordon*, Stephen King gives us nine-year-old Trisha McFarland who gets lost in the woods because she petulantly stomps away from her mother to relieve herself. It's such a simple, human response we easily identify with it. That's how King draws us into his lead character's crisis.

Sympathy intensifies the reader's emotional investment in the lead. There are some simple ways to establish sympathy:

1. Imminent Trouble

Put the hero in terrible, imminent trouble and you've got the sympathy factor at work right away. In *Tom Gordon*, Trisha is lost in dangerous woods after she stomps away. That's immediate, physical jeopardy.

Jeopardy can also be emotional. Dean Koontz often uses this device. In *Midnight*, FBI agent Sam Booker is close to an emotional abyss. His teenage son hates him, and he is fighting to find reasons to keep on living. He is in emotional jeopardy. Part of the depth of the book come from his finding reasons to carry on.

2. Hardship

If the lead has to face some misfortune in life, not of her own making, sympathy abounds. In *The Winner*, David Baldacci gives us a poor, Southern woman who grew up without love, education or good hygiene (even her teeth are bad!) So when she takes steps to overcome her state of affairs, we are rooting for her.

3. The Underdog

America loves people who face long odds. John Grisham has used the underdog in many of his books. One of his best, *The Rainmaker*, is the classic David and Goliath story switched to the courtroom. We can't help but root for Rudy Baylor as he battles a huge defense firm.

4. Vulnerability

Readers worry about a lead who might be crushed at any time. In *Rose Madder*, Stephen King follows a battered wife who, after years in a hellish marriage, finally gets up the courage to run away from her psychopathic cop-husband. But she is so naive about the ways of the world, and her husband so good at tracking people down, we worry about her from the moment she steps out the door.

The next dynamic of lead character bond is likability. A likable lead, not surprisingly, is someone who does likable things. They do favors for people. Or they are witty in conversation. They are not selfish. They have an expansive view of life. These are people we like to be around. Think about people you like, and then incorporate some of those characteristics into your lead.

Finally, inner conflict pulls the reader into the emotional struggle of the lead. Inner conflict is nothing more than a fight between two opposing emotions. Many times it is fear on one side, telling the lead not to act. Inner conflict is resolved when the lead, by listening to the other side — duty, honor, principle or the like — overcomes fear and acts accordingly.

If you use these elements well you will have the first building block of solid novel locked in—a lead readers care about and want to follow.

O is for Objective

Back to our "Will Work for Food" guy. What if he tossed down his sign, put a parachute on his back, and started climbing the Empire State Building?

Interest zooms. Why?

This character has an objective.

Sol Stein, the legendary editor and writing teacher, says his number one rule for a story is, "Somebody has to want something badly." Find that something for your lead and your readers will be hooked.

An objective can take either of two forms: to GET something, or to GET AWAY from something.

• *The Girl Who Loved Tom Gordon* is about a girl who desperately wants to get back to civilization.

• In *Jaws*, Brody desperately wants to get the shark.

• In *Rose Madder*, Rose wants to get away from her psycho husband.

• In *The Firm*, Mitch McDeere wants to get away from the Mafia.

Solid stories have one, and only one, dominant objective for the lead character. This forms the "story question"—will the lead realize her objective?

Further, that objective has to be essential to the well-being of the lead. If the lead doesn't get it (or get away from it), her life will take a tremendous hit for the worse.

Here are a few hints on making that objective crucial.

If the objective is related to staying alive, that always fits the bill. Most suspense novels have the threat of death hanging over the lead from the start. Death can also hang over others—Clarice Starling in *The Silence of the Lambs* is driven to stop Buffalo Bill before he kills another innocent victim.

Not all objectives have to involve death, however. The essential thing is that it is crucial to that lead's sense of well-being.

Consider Oscar in Neil Simon's play, *The Odd Couple*. He is a very happy slob. Nothing pleases him more than smoky poker games in his apartment, and not cleaning up afterward. He takes in his suicidal friend, Felix, out of compassion. But Felix is a clean nut. Eventually, this drives Oscar crazy. If he doesn't get rid of Felix, his happy life as a slob will be ruined! The story works because Simon establishes just how important the slob life is to Oscar.

C is for Confrontation

Now our human fly is halfway up the Empire State Building. We already know he's interesting because he has an objective, and with a little imagination, you can think up a reason why this is crucial to his well-being.

Is there anything we can do to ratchet up the engrossment level?

Yes! New York City cops are trying to stop him! They have plans to nab him around floor 65. Worse yet, one of their snipers on the roof of another building has him in his sights, because the police mistakenly believe he's a terrorist with a bomb. And what about the big thunderstorm that moves in and starts pouring sheets of icy rain all over our hero?

Suddenly, things are a lot more interesting.

The reason is confrontation. Opposition from characters and outside forces makes your story fully alive. If your lead moves toward her objective without anything in her way, we deprive readers of what they secretly want: Worry! Readers want to fret about the lead, keeping an intense emotional involvement all the way through the novel.

Some wise old scribe once put it this way: "Get your protagonist up a tree. Throw rocks at him. Then get him down."

Throwing rocks means putting obstacles in your lead's way. Making things tough on her. Never let her off easy.

How do you know what obstacles to throw? The first step is to conceive an opposition character. I use this term rather than "villain," because the opposition does not have to be evil. The opposition merely has to have a compelling reason to stop the lead.

Three keys will help you come up with good opposition:

• Make the opposition a person. (A master like Stephen King can make the opposition non-personal, as in Tom Gordon, where it's Trisha against the woods. But don't try this at home.)

• If it is a group, like the law firm in The Rainmaker, select one person in that group to take the lead role for the opposition.

• Make the opposition stronger than the lead. If the opposition can be easily matched, why should the reader worry?

• Ask: Why do I love my opposition character? Climbing into the opposition's skin will give you an empathetic view, and a better character as a result.

Your confrontation still needs one more crucial ingredient: adhesive. Because if your lead can simply walk away from the opponent, and still be able to realize her objective, the reader will be asking, "Well, why doesn't she?"

An adhesive is any strong relationship or circumstance that holds people together.

Duty is a strong adhesive. A cop who is assigned a case has a duty to solve it. A lawyer has a duty to represent his client. A mother has a moral duty to a child.

Obsession is another adhesive. In *Rose Madder*, the psycho husband is not going to stop hunting down his wife. He's obsessed with seeing her dead.

Another adhesive is physical surrounding. In Stephen King's *The Shining*, the Torrance family is stuck in a ghostly hotel that is completely snowed in. Dean Koontz places everyone in *Icebound* on an iceberg, with no way out.

So you must figure out a reason why the lead and opposition can't withdraw from the action.

Writing your novel now is a matter of recording various scenes of confrontation, each ending with some sort of setback for your lead, forcing her to analyze her situation anew and take some other action toward her objective.

Think of the long middle of your book as a series of increasingly intense battles. Sometimes your lead will be out of action to regroup, but most of the time she'll be fighting toward her ultimate goal.

Back and forth, parry and thrust.

That's the heart of your novel.

K is for Knockout

Will our human fly make it? Whatever the answer, readers will want to know for sure.

I once asked an old sports writer why he thought boxing was so popular. He smacked his fist into his hand. "Pow!" he said, letting his arm fall like a sack of potatoes.

It is for the knockout people watch boxing, he explained. They'll accept a decision, but prefer to see one fighter kissing the canvas. What they hate is a draw. That doesn't satisfy anyone.

Readers of commercial fiction want to see a knockout at the end. A literary novel can play with a bit more ambiguity. In either case, the ending must have knockout power. As the great writing teacher Dwight Swain once said, "A strong ending may save a weak story. If the ending disappoints, on the other hand, the reader quite possibly will feel that the story as a whole is a failure."

So take your lead through the journey toward her objective, and then send the opposition to the mat. Here are a few tips to help you do just that.

The most exciting boxing matches are those where it looks like one fighter is going to lose, only to draw on reserves of strength to deliver a knockout blow to his opponent.

Do that with your novel. Maintain the tension in the story until the last possible moment. As you near the end it should look as if the opposition is the one who will win. He has everything going for him. The lead is up against the ropes.

Only when the lead reaches deep within and makes her move will the knockout blow be thrown.

Near the ending you want the readers to ask, *Will the lead fight or run away? Will the forces marshaled against the lead simply be too much for her to face?*

To stay and fight, your lead will have to call upon moral or physical courage.

- In *Jaws*, Brody must finally head out to sea and, with help, kill the shark. He does.

- In *The Rainmaker*, Rudy must go all the way through a trial even though he has no experience. He wins.

- In Dean Koontz's *Intensity*, Chyna must find a way to kill her tormentor. She finds it.

- In *The Silence of the Lambs*, Clarice stays with the case in order to stop Buffalo Bill. She stops him.

Readers prefer to have the opposing force defeated decisively by the hero. But that doesn't always have to be the case.

A good example is Jonathan Harr's *A Civil Action,* a non-fiction book that reads better than most legal thrillers. It tells the story of lawyer Jan Schlichtmann's obsession to get justice for the residents of small town whose water supply was poisoned by two huge companies. Of course, the other side, with unlimited funds, does everything to crush him, personally and professionally. They do. But we are left with a sense of awe at how long the hero stood up under the gun.

There is one more thing you need to do to leave the reader with the ultimate reading experience. I call these the "Ah" and the "Uh-Oh."

You get the "ah" once the main action of the story is wrapped up. With the knockout blow administered, you can now give us a final scene in which something from the hero's personal life is resolved.

In *Midnight*, Sam Booker has brought down the evil plan of the villain. But the book ends with Sam returning to try and make amends with his rebellious son. Sam embraces him, and even though the issues aren't resolved, at least the process has begun. "That was the wonderful thing," goes the book's last line. "It had begun."

This emotional resolution in the lead's personal life makes us go "ah." It's like the perfect last note in a great piece of music. Look at the very last scenes in a number of thrillers and you'll see how often this is done.

Or, a book can leave us with a sense of foreboding, with the reader uttering, "uh-oh." Charles Wilson's *Embryo* has such an ending. The book details the search for a mad doctor and the process he uses to bring forth children outside the womb. They become children who are evil, who actually smile when contemplating how bad they can be.

The main story is resolved when the hero and love interest end up with what they think is a normal child. All is well. But in the final scene their little girl, Pauline, is alone outside. She finds some matches and, curious, lights one. She pitches it and it lands on her dog's back.

> He suddenly jumped and whirled and tried to look back across his shoulder at what had stung him. Pauline realized what she had done and looked sad for a moment.
> And then she smiled.

Uh-oh!

Wilson has cleverly left us to contemplate the horror starting all over again.

You can always find an "ah" or an "uh-oh" ending for your novel. It's worth it.

So if you want to keep selling novels, knock 'em out at the end.

The LOCK System is truly magical in its effects. Follow it, and your novel can't help but be solidly structured. You can then spend your time pouring your voice and imagination into the pages. You'll be free from worry about form so you can concentrate on content.

The Three Act Structure

A story well told has a beginning, muddle, and end.

Yes, I meant to write *muddle*. Because that's what Act II is all about — trouble.

It's deceptively simple yet exceedingly powerful.

Why does it work?

It's natural. We live and think in three acts.

We are born and have a childhood (Act I). We live our lives and do our things and face our problems (Act II). Then (if all goes well) we reach old age and finally get to the fade out (Act III).

We wake up in the morning. We spend the bulk of the day at work or doing personal things. In the evening we get ready for bed (exciting life, isn't it?)

Then we're given a problem to solve, say at work. Getting the problem is Act I, thinking about a solution and trying things out is Act II, and finally we succeed — or fail — in Act II.

So it's no wonder that readers respond best to stories that follow the three acts. Structure is therefore crucial if you hope to sell a lot of books. There are some voices out there who preach that structure should be ignored when writing fiction. Just play and pour yourself out on the page!

That may be good advice for therapy, but it's terrible advice for the author who wishes to make money. The latter is all about connecting with readers, and readers are wired for solid structure. They are frustrated or, worse, bored with novels that don't have it.

So have it.

Which means study it. On that score let me recommend *Structuring Your Novel* by K. M. Weiland and my own *Plot & Structure*.

16. How to Write a Novel in a Month

I extol the virtues of National Novel Writing Month, or NaNoWriMo for short. The novel I wrote in November of 2010 was one I had under contract. It became, after editing of course, *The Year of Eating Dangerously* (under my pen name, K. Bennett).

There are similar stories. Hugh Howey wrote his novella *Wool* during that same NaNo year. The dang thing sold in the hundreds of thousands as an ebook, and got optioned by Ridley Scott. Howey then entered a *print only* deal with a major publisher for lots of money.

Howey's case is a lightning strikes once or twice kind of thing, and most writers are not going to have that kind of out-of-the-gate success. But that's beside the NaNo point. The point is to get your story down fast, and unleash the writer within. It's to give you a sense of the value of finishing an entire novel (even though it will need massive editing).

As the great Robert B. Parker said, "A writer's job is to produce." NaNo is one month of pure production.

Here are ten tips to help you write a novel in a month. Even if you don't do the official NaNo, you can still follow these steps to get to an editable first draft in a fast and efficient way.

Notice the keyword *editable*. You're not finished when the month is over. You'll have a novel, yes, and that's a good thing. But do not, I repeat, do not send it anywhere yet. As industry observer Tom Mitchell put it, "NaNoWriMo must be the worst thing that's happened to literary agents since alcoholic lunches fell out of fashion." What he means is that agents, sadly, get inundated with manuscripts and proposals in the December after NaNoWriMo.

First you write.

Then you fix.

1. Take a week to plan

Use one week for creative brainstorming and organizing. You should never start out with a blank slate. A few,simple steps will get you to a much stronger story. Use my LOCK System (explained in the previous chapter) in the following way:

• Spend a day brainstorming about your lead character's backstory, goals and dreams. What is it about your lead that will make readers want to keep reading?

• Be sure that the story objective involves some form of death: physical, professional or psychological. Take a day to brainstorm reasons your Lead will have to be involved. Think about moral or professional duty as a possible motivation.

• Spend a day on your opposition character. Remember, the opponent does not have to be evil, just have an opposing agenda (think Tommy Lee Jones in *The Fugitive*). However, if you do want to use a villain, be fair to him. Justify his actions (at least in his own mind). Don't create a stereotype. Write out some backstory on the opposition character that explains why he is the way he is.

• This will no doubt be subject to change as your novel develops, but it's good to have a destination in mind. How do you want the reader to feel at the end? Will your Lead be victorious? Sacrificial? Spend a day messing around with actual scene possibilities for the climax. Choose one as your "go to" scene, knowing you can toss it out as the novel progresses.

• Take an hour or two just to brainstorm scenes. This step is the most fun for me. With a stack of 3 x 5 cards I go to Starbucks and settle in. I let scene ideas occur to me at random and jot them on the cards. I put just enough on a card to know what happens. I want to be able to visualize it. I don't worry about putting these scenes in any kind of order. Yet.

Once I have a good stack of cards, maybe 30 or 40, I take a break. Then at home I divide them into three stacks according to the three-act structure.

• Let this story material sit for a day as you plan your writing schedule. Look at your calendar and block out every free chunk you can. Determine to cut as many distractions as possible during the writing month. DVR favorite shows. Put an auto-responder

on your email. Explain to friends that you're taking
time off. Go on a "social media" diet.

2. Choose mood music

Create some playlists of soundtracks and songs
that create the right mood for your story, as well as
music to pump you up. I have an "Energy to Write"
list that is full of upbeat rock and movie music. I blast
that sometimes to get my blood racing to write. Then,
for specific scenes, I'll put on some soundtracks. For
example, if I'm writing suspense I have a slate of
music from Alfred Hitchcock movies.

Some writers say they need silence to write. That's
fine. Try the music *before* you write.

3. Watch a "movie in your mind" the night before the month begins

On the night before you start, plan to get a good
night's sleep. Before bed get to a quiet spot, a
comfortable chair. Put your mood music on softly
and close your eyes. Now let a "movie" happen in
your mind. Watch your story unfold. Don't force
anything. Let scenes happen, nudge your characters
but never push them.

When you go to bed, tell the boys in the basement
to work hard while you snooze.

4. Kill that first day

Make the very first day the most productive day
of your writing life. NaNoWriMo works out to an

average of just over 1600 words a day. Try to blast past it on Day 1. It will give your confidence a boost.

5. Make it your goal to begin each day with a "furious 500"

Try getting 500 words down the very first thing in the morning (or second, after you start the coffee brewing). If you have to get up half an hour earlier, so be it.

6. Jot down notes just before you go to sleep

Take five minutes (that's all you'll need) before you go to sleep to put down a few notes about what you might write the next day. Think one or two scenes ahead. If you're feeling stuck, ask this key question: "How can I make things harder on my characters?"

7. Stick to the knitting

By that I mean the main plot. Make this your focus of attention. At 50,000 words, a NaNo novel is short, and cannot support multiple plotlines.

If you find yourself coming up with a subplot idea, jot a few notes and set it aside for a day or two while you're on your main plot. If another idea occurs to you, jot that one down, too. After a few days, assess the subplots and choose one, only one. The best one. The one with the most possibilities for conflict. Integrate a scene or two. Then press on.

If you use Scrivener, you can color code the subplot scenes to keep track of them. One subplot only!

8. Write a 200 word nightcap

That is, find some time in the evening to write at least 200 more words. That's not many. This is in addition to the words you write during the day. If you do a furious 500 first thing in the morning, and a 200 word nightcap, you've done almost half the words you need for your daily quota.

9. Break off in the middle of sentence

That's an old Hemingway trick. And he won the Nobel Prize. Stop your writing stint right in the middle of a sentence. When you sit down to it the next day, you'll be in flow.

10. If you get stuck

You will probably come to a few points where you don't know what to write next. Fear will grip you like the cold hands of a clumsy proctologist. You don't want to waste too much time in fretting over this, so: open a dictionary at random. Find the first noun you see on the left hand page. Start writing something, anything, based on what the noun brings to your mind.

If you're still stuck, re-watch *Misery* and imagine that your number one fan insists that you finish by the end of the month.

Even if you fall short of your novel writing goal, you will have taken great strides in becoming a more productive writer. And if you want to write for a living that's what you've got to be.

Now that you've got a first draft, what do you do with it?

You can start by reading — or re-reading — the next chapter.

17. How to Self-Edit Your Novel

I've written an entire book on self-editing. I hear from writers all the time that it is their "bible" when it comes to the revision process. I love being able to help. And while the complete scope of that book cannot be reproduced here, let me at least lay out a process for you.

First, I want to talk a little bit about your *voice*. This is an extremely important part of your personal style. Readers respond to voice. It will make your books that much more attractive.

Finding Your Unique Voice

You hear it every time there's a panel of agents and/or editors, when they are asked what they're looking for in a manuscript. Someone always says, "A fresh voice."

But no one knows how to define it. Over the years I've heard some attempts at explanation, and I've jotted them down. Here they are:

- A combination of character, setting, page turning.
- A distinctive style, like a Sergio Leone film.
- It's who you are.
- Personality on the page.
- It's something written from your deepest truth.
- Your expression as an artist.

Well, okay. I guess. But how do we develop voice? Indeed, is it something that can be developed? Or is it something you're born with?

What if you write in different genres? Is your voice in a noir thriller going to be the same as your voice in a romance?

Should writers even worry about voice? I counsel my students to be true to the story they're telling, true to the characters, and not to worry about this elusive thing everyone says they want. If the tale is well told, that's the main thing.

But I do think there is something to be said for trying to coax out a little more voice, even though you can never quite nail it down to pure technique.

So what is it that does the coaxing? In a word, joy.

> In the great story-tellers, there is a sort of self-enjoyment in the exercise of the sense of narrative; and this, by sheer contagion, communicates enjoyment to the reader. Perhaps it may be called (by analogy with the familiar phrase, "the joy of living") the joy of telling tales. The joy of telling tales which shines through Treasure Island is perhaps the main reason for

181

the continued popularity of the story. The author is having such a good time in telling his tale that he gives us necessarily a good time in reading it.
- Clayton Meeker Hamilton, *A Manual of the Art of Fiction* (1919)

I think Professor Hamilton nailed it. When an author is joyous in his telling, it pulses through the words. When you read a Ray Bradbury, for instance, you sense his joy. He was in love with words and his own imagination, and it showed.

I recall a *Writer's Digest* fiction column by Lawrence Block, back in the 80s, and he was telling about being at a book signing with some other authors, one of whom was a guy named Stephen King. And Stephen King's line was longer by far than for any of the other guys.

Which got Larry to thinking, what was it about King's stuff? And he decided that it was this joy aspect. When you read Stephen King, you feel like you're reading an author who loves writing, loves making up tales to creep us out, enjoys the very act of setting words down on paper.

Because when you're joyful in the writing, the writing is fresher and fuller. Fuller of what? Of you. And that translates to the page and becomes that thing called Voice.

So the question is, how can you get more joy into your writing?

Here are some thoughts:

1. Be excited about your story. If you're not jazzed about what you're writing, you can't be joyful

182

about writing it. Dwight Swain, the great writing teacher, once said that the secret of excitement is to go deeper into your characters. Create more backstory, more secrets, more complexity, and you'll get excited again.

2. Write at your peak "freshness" time. Find out when you're most creative and awake and alive. Write for all you're worth during that time.

3. Take a break when it's drudgery, and do something else for a while. I find that if I read a passage by one of my favorite writers, I soon enough get excited about writing and want to go back to my project.

4. When you write, write. Let loose. Let go. Feel it. Go for it. Create white hot material. That's what you want to work with when it comes time to edit.

The Editing Process

You finished your first draft.

This is cause for celebration. There are a lot of wannabe writers out there, but many (most?) of them never push through and write a book.

Celebrate with a favorite meal, champagne, loved one, spouse, dog, whatever.

And don't think about your book for three weeks.

That's what I said.

During this interval be developing your next book.

Always have a next book.

Okay, after three weeks you're ready to do a self-edit job.

I like to print out a hard copy. The reason is it's easier for me to make notes on a page. Some people read on their ereader. That's fine, but not quite as flexible.

The point is to read your draft through in as little time as possible. Read it as if you were someone who'd never heard of you, the author, and is taking a chance on this book.

The First Read Through

Take minimal notes and do not, whatever you do, pause for substantial editing! You are looking for an overview, a big picture of your story. You want to know if it moves and you want to spot (and mark) the dull parts.

As you read, pretend your manuscript is in the hands of a tired New York acquisitions editor. Her job is to find a smashing good book for her publisher. She's on the subway heading back to Brooklyn. It's the end of a long day. She figures she'll use the time to take a look at one more manuscript. Yours.

Ask yourself, with every page, is this a place where that editor might be tempted to put the manuscript aside?

Keep an eye on your characters. Are they believable? Are they doing believable things? I like what the writer Stanley Schmidt once said: "At every significant juncture in a story, consciously look at the situation from the viewpoint of every character involved – and let each of them make the best move they can from his or her own point of view."

Are the stakes high enough? I mentioned in an earlier chapter that the stakes must be death: personal, professional, psychological — or a mix of all of them with one predominant.

The Second Draft

Now you do your heavy edit, doing the best you can to fix the things you think need fixing.

This is a hard part, but it's invaluable training. You get stronger as an author the more you go through this process.

Just do the best you can.

Get the draft all nice and spell checked.

And now show it to:

Five Beta Readers

You now need five beta readers. Do a little research and put in a little effort, and you'll get a quality group together. (See my earlier discussion of beta readers and editors in the chapter Secrets of a Winning System.)

Four out of the five need to tell you they really liked your book. They don't have to love it, though that would be the best result. But they have to more than like it. They have to really like it.

These are your scientific categories:

1. Loved it!

2. Really liked it!

3. Liked it.

4. Only okay.

5. Dreadful.

6. Don't ever ask me to read anything of yours again.

7. I am getting a restraining order against you.

Your book needs to score a 1 or a 2 from four out of the five readers.

Is that a high standard? You bet it is. Because if you want to be a name brand and not the generic, if you truly want to write for a living, you've got to go through your paces.

Take all their suggestions and comments to heart. Think about your book. Make the changes you think need to be made.

Professional Edits

Now it's time to turn your book over to a good content editor (sometimes called a developmental editor). This is the costliest part of the whole process, but you need to look at it as a business investment in your product — which is you.

There is no better way to grow as a writer than to have a good editor work with you. See my discussion on editors in the chapter A Short Course on Self-Publishing. Once you've got a few novels under your belt you may begin to feel confident in letting the beta readers handle the developmental edits. You are then left with line editing and proofreading for the final steps.

It used to be said that it took five novels for the traditionally published author to build a significant following. And I say it usually takes five novels that follow this self-editing process for a writer to begin to feel like a true professional.

It's a long haul, but it's worth it. The dividends will be paid out for the rest of your career.

18. The 5 Biggest Fiction Writing Mistakes

The best fiction writers write like they're in love—and edit like they're in charge.

First drafting should be a wild and wonderful ride, full of discovery, dreams, and promises. But at some point you have to settle down and make the book actually work. You need to approach your manuscript with sober objectivity and knowledge of the craft.

Having seen many hundreds of manuscripts over the years, I've identified five mistakes that regularly turn up. Fixing them will immediately elevate your novel above the ever growing mountain of slush.

1. Happy People in Happy Land

One of the most common problems I see, especially in the opening chapter, is a scene presenting characters who are perfectly happy in their ordinary world. The writer thinks that by showing us nice people doing nice things, readers will care about these pleasant folk when they're finally hit with a problem!

Readers engage with plot via trouble, threat, change, or challenge. I call this the opening disturbance. It can be stunning, as in Jodi Picoult's Lone Wolf, which begins:

> Seconds before our truck slams into the tree, I remember the first time I tried to save a life.

Or it can be something quieter, a single item that is "off kilter," as in the opening of Sarah Pekkanen's The Opposite of Me:

> As I pulled open the heavy glass door of Richards, Dunne & Krantz and walked down the long hallway toward the executive offices, I noticed a light was on up ahead.
>
> Lights were never on this early.

And as your novel progresses, be on the lookout for long stops in Happy Land.

During the final edit of my novel, *Don't Leave Me,* I noticed one scene where my Lead, Chuck Samson, still recovering from his wife's death, goes with his autistic brother to a fellow teacher's apartment for dinner. Chuck used to do magic when his wife was alive. Stan wants him to do a trick. Chuck resists but is cajoled into it. In the original version he did a "disappearing knife" trick successfully, and everyone was pleased until the cops arrived at the door at the end of the scene.

Too much happy. What was the solution? Chuck blows it:

> Chuck placed both his hands over the knife, slid it toward him and off the table into his lap. He kept the motion smooth and put his hands up to his mouth and pretended like he was swallowing the knife.
>
> But as he did the knife slid off his lap and hit the floor with a clank.
>
> "Oops," Stan said.
>
> Chuck had not blown that trick in twenty years. He looked at his hands like they were foreign objects that had betrayed him.
>
> Wendy laughed good-naturedly. But when Chuck looked at her, she stopped laughing.

Trouble is your business. Make more of it.

2. A World Without Fear

The best novels, the ones that stay with you all the way to the end—and beyond—have death hanging over every scene.

As we talked about earlier, death comes in three forms (physical, professional, psychological). When death on the line fear should be felt throughout. Fear is a continuum. It can be simple worry or outright terror. You can put it everywhere. And should.

In the pulp classic *The Red Scarf* by Gil Brewer, the main character's schemes are closing in around him (as usually happens in noir). His wife is trying to have a normal dinner with him. But he's worried:

> "Come on and eat, Roy. Supper's ready."
>
> "All right." I went into the kitchen and sat down and stared at my plate. I didn't want to eat. There was this rotten black feeling all through me and I couldn't shake it.
>
> "Eat something, Roy. What's the matter?"
>
> "Nothing. I just don't feel so hot."
>
> I wanted to go over and take this guy Radan and knock the hell out of him. Only I knew I wouldn't. You know when it's not ready. You know something's going to happen.
>
> Something had to happen. It was like before a big storm, with the black clouds out there on the horizon. Everything goes calm and dead, and then...

Once the story is underway, scenes where fear is not present in some form means the stakes are not high enough or the characters aren't acting the way they should in the face of death.

Put more fear in your scenes.

3. Marshmallow Dialogue

Dialogue is the fastest way to improve a manuscript. And to sink it. When an agent, editor, or reader sees crisp, tension-filled dialogue, they gain immediate confidence in the writer's ability.

But when the dialogue is sodden and undistinguished, it has the opposite effect. I call this marshmallow dialogue.

Pro dialogue is compressed. Marshmallow dialogue is puffy.

Pro dialogue has conflict. Marshmallow dialogue is too sweet.

Pro dialogue sounds different for each character. Marshmallow dialogue sounds the same.

Fortunately, the fixes are easy.

First, make sure you can "hear" every character in a distinct voice. Use a Voice Journal. This is a free-form document in a character's voice, talking to you, the author, on a variety of topics. Develop this document until the character sounds unique.

Second, compress your dialogue as much as possible. Cut words, and sometimes even dialogue itself. Here's an example:

> "Mary, are you angry with me?" John asked.
> "You are damn straight that I'm mad at you," Mary said.
> "But why? You have got absolutely no reason to be!"
> "Oh but I do, I do. And you can see it in my face, can't you?"

Now the alternative:

"You angry with me?" John asked.
"Damn straight," Mary said.
"You got no reason to be!"
Mary felt her hands curling into fists.

Try this: copy a lengthy dialogue exchange into a fresh document. Then cut and compress as much as you can. Compare it to the original. Nine times out of ten you will prefer all or part of the new version.

Finally, be sure to include some sort of tension in every dialogue exchange. Remember fear? At the very least you can have some aspect of fear (worry, anxiety, fright) going on inside one of the characters so that communication is partially impaired.

And heat up the different agendas each character has in a scene. Let them use dialogue as a weapon to get what they want.

Dialogue is *sooo* important to fiction success that I wrote an entire book on the subject, How to Write Dazzling Dialogue.

4. Predictability

Remember, readers like to worry about characters in crisis. They want to tremble about what's around the next corner (emotional or physical). If a reader knows what's coming, and it does, the worry factor is blown. Your novel no longer conveys a fictive dream but a dull ride down familiar streets.

The fix is simple: put something unexpected in every scene. Doing this one thing keeps the reader on edge.

So how do you come up with the unexpected?

You make lists.

You pause and ask yourself what might happen next, and you make a list of possibilities. Don't grab the first thing that comes to your mind. You usually jump to clichés. Force yourself to list at least five possibilities, maybe more.

Make lists around three primary areas:

- Description
- Action
- Dialogue

Dump generic description for something unique to the character's perceptions. How might he see a room where someone died? What's one surprising thing about the wallpaper? The bed? The closet?

Action: Close your eyes and watch your scene unfold. Let the characters improvise. What are some things they do that are far out? If something looks interesting, justify it.

Dialogue: Don't always use "on the nose" exchanges. How might characters say things that put other characters (and thus, the reader) off balance? From Clarice Starling's first conversation with Hannibal Lecter in *The Silence of the Lambs:*

> "I think you've been destructive. For me it's the same thing."

"Evil's just destructive?
Then storms are evil, if it's
just that simple. And we have
fire, and then there's hail.
Underwriters lump it all under
'Acts of God.'"
"Deliberate—"
"I collect church collapses,
recreationally. Did you see the
recent one in Sicily?"

You can make these lists in your planning stages,
just before writing a scene, or when you revise.

5. Lost Love

As I said up front, a book idea is like falling in
love. Outlining and planning are the wooing. Writing
the novel is your commitment to marriage (which
would make writing the opening scenes the
honeymoon).

But sometime in there the writer and book will
need some marriage counseling. If you lose the verve
for your material, it will show up on the page.

So how do you regain lost love? The surest way is
by going deeper into your characters.

Start with backstory. Maybe you've already done
an extensive bio for your main character. Try starting
a new one. Use some of the old material if you like,
but put in plenty that's new.

Focus on the year your character turned sixteen.
That's a pivotal year for all of us. Create a detailed
account of what happened at that crucial stage. What

incident shaped her life? What were the romances, heartaches, tragedies? Write some scenes in detail about that year.

Do this for your antagonist, too, and your secondary characters. Soon enough you'll be excited to get back to your story.

Next focus on what your Lead yearns for. Why do we yearn? Because we feel a lack, a need, a hole in our soul.

So yearning is about connection. This, in fact, is the power of myth. Joseph Campbell taught that myths were a way of gaining connection to something transcendent, a life source, an essential mystery.

And readers, too, yearn for connection—with books they can get lost in and be moved by. Fix these five areas in your work, and your books can be among them.

19. How to Write a Novella

Novellas are back. Once a staple of the old pulp era, the novella was a form that pretty much had dried up in traditional publishing.

That's because the trim size of this smaller book led readers to feel they weren't getting an entire fiction experience. And the publishers had to price them high enough to make a profit.

Which is too bad, because a novella (like a short story) can often provide a powerhouse reading experience that is the equal of a great novel.

A novella is not really, as some say "like a novel, only shorter." It is its own form. Although there are some quibbles, the general view is that a novella is between 20k and 40k words. Less than that is a novelette or story; more than that is a novel (though a 45k novel is kinda chintzy).

Novellas provide a self-publishing author a way to get more material out there in a short period of time.

Remember, this is a quality and quantity game. So if you're a fiction writer, consider novellas as part of your list.

The following are general guidelines for writing a novella. I say general because, like all writing tips, they are subject to change. But *only* if you have a good reason for the exception.

1. One plot

The length of the novella dictates that it have one plot. It's too short to support subplots. That doesn't mean you don't have *plot complications*. It's just that you are doing your dance around one story problem.

2. One POV

It's almost always best to stick with one point of view. My novellas, like *Watch Your Back* and *One More Lie,* are written in first person POV. That's because you want, in the short space you have, to create as intimate a relationship between the Lead character and the reader as possible.

As indicated earlier, more than one POV is acceptable *if you have a reason for including it.* And that reason is NOT so you can fill more pages.

A modern master of the novella is, of course, Stephen King. A look at his collection, *Different Seasons,* reveals three novellas written in first person POV. The exception is *Apt Pupil,* which is about an ex-Nazi's influence over a thirteen-year-old boy. The story thus has a reason for shifting between these two points of view. However, I note that *Apt Pupil* is the longest of these, and I actually suspect it's over 40k words, making it a short novel.

3. One central question

There is one story question per novella, usually in the form: Will X get Y?

In *Rita Hayworth and the Shawshank Redemption,* by Stephen King, the question is, will the wrongly convicted Andy Dufresne survive in God-awful Shawshank prison?

In *The Old Man and the Sea:* Will the old fisherman, Santiago, land the big fish?

A Christmas Carol: Will Ebenezer Scrooge get redemption?

4. One style and tone

There are novels that crack the style barrier in various ways, but a novella should stick to one tone, one style throughout.

In the old pulp days, novellas were common and usually written in the hard boiled style.

My two novellas mentioned above are done in the confessional style of James M. Cain—the narrator looking back at his past sins, detailing the consequences of same, with a twist ending.

Romance would have a different tone. Ditto paranormal. Whatever the genre, keep it consistent.

Pricing a Novella

The pricing issue is one that is never entirely settled. It's not an exact science.

If you're just starting out and trying to establish a readership, go for the low price point of 99¢.

If you're writing a series in novella form (this was how *Wool* by Hugh Howey took off), you can try this: make the first on perma-free and the others $2.99.

I would not go over $2.99 as the price of a novella.

Some Famous Novellas

The Pearl, John Steinbeck

The Old Man and the Sea, Ernest Hemingway

A Christmas Carol, Charles Dickens

The Body, Stephen King

Rita Hayworth and the Shawshank Redemption, Stephen King

The Escape Route, Rod Serling

Double Indemnity, James M. Cain

A River Runs Through It, Norman Maclean

Phantom Lady, William Irish (aka Cornell Woolrich)

20. How to Write a Short Story

Short stories are a nice way to draw in potential long-term readers. They can be offered for free or 99¢ (it's insane to charge more than that). My strategy is to use short stories to gain new readers (and here FREE works particularly well) and also to put together an eventual collection. A collection can carry a higher price point.

But here's a little word of warning: I find short stories to be the most difficult form in all of fiction. But done well it is highly rewarding for you as a writer, and sometimes a writer has to write for love.

A novelist friend recently asked, What is it that defines a short story? What's the key to writing one? How is it different from a novel or novella?

I pondered that for a while, and one day I woke up thinking, *A short story is about one shattering moment.*

Could it really be so? What about the different genres? There are literary short stories (Raymond Carver), but also horror (Stephen King), science fiction (Harlan Ellison), crime (Jeffery Deaver), and

201

the like. They couldn't all be about one shattering moment, could they?

I decided to have a cheeseburger and forget the whole thing.

But the boys would not let me drop it. And now I think they're right (as usual). So let's take it apart.

When I took a writing workshop with one of the recognized masters of the modern short story, Raymond Carver, I found his genius lay in the "telling detail," a way to illuminate, with a minimalist image or line of dialogue, a shattering emotional moment in the life of a character.

The story we studied in his workshop was "Will You Please Be Quiet, Please?" A married couple, middle class with two young kids, has a conversation one night. The wife brings up an incident at a party a couple of years before. Slowly, we realize she needs to confess something, needs to be forgiven. She'd slept with another man that night. That is the shattering moment in the story, the husband's realization of what his wife did.

This happens in the middle. The rest of the story is about the emotional aftermath of that moment. Thus, the structure of the story looks like this:

This is the same structure as Hemingway's classic, "Hills Like White Elephants." In this story about a couple conversing at a train station, the shattering moment occurs inside the woman. It's when she accedes to her boyfriend's desire that she have an abortion (amazingly, the word *abortion* is never used in the story). We see what's happened to her almost entirely via dialogue. In fact, she has a line much like the husband's in the Carver story. She says, "Would you please please please please please please please stop talking?"

We know at the end of both these stories that the characters will never be the same, that life for them has been ineluctably altered. That's what a shattering moment does.

Structurally, this moment can come at the end of the story. When it works, it's like an emotional bomb going off. Two literary stories that do this are "The Swimmer" by John Cheever and "Where Are You Going, Where Have You Been?" by Joyce Carol Oates. That structure looks like this:

Now let's move to the genre short story. Here, the same idea applies. The shattering moment is usually one that is outside (i.e., a plot moment) as opposed to inside (i.e., a character moment). Often, that moment is a "twist" at the end of the story. The most famous example is, no doubt, O. Henry's "The Gift of the Magi."

Jeffery Deaver is a master of this type (see his collections *Twisted* and *More Twisted*.) Get your hands on his story "Chapter and Verse" (from *More Twisted*) to see what I mean. It's one of my favorites.

My recent crime short story, "Autumnal," follows this pattern as well. We think the story is going one way, but at the end it is quite another.

This is also the structure most often used in *The Twilight Zone*. Think about some of the classic episodes:

"To Serve Man." Remember the shattering shout at the end? "It's a cook book!"

"Time Enough at Last." Always voted the most memorable episode, because of its heartbreaking twist at the end. This is the one where the loner with the thick glasses emerges after nuclear war has killed everyone, but now has time enough at last to read all the books he wants. And then . . .

"The Eye of the Beholder." This one blew me away as a kid. It's the one where the surgeons, in shadows all the way through, are working to save the disfigured face of a patient. One of the all-time great twists.

This pattern is just like the one described above, in literary short stories, only now it's a shattering *plot* twist at the end:

And, you guessed it, you can also do a story with the shattering moment somewhere in the opening pages, and work out the aftermath for the rest of the tale. Lawrence Block's "A Candle for the Bag Lady" is like that (You can find this story in Block's collection, *Enough Rope*). The structure looks like this:

So there you have it. If you want to write a short story, find that moment that is emotionally life-changing, or craftily plot-twisting. Then write everything around that moment. Structurally, it's simple to understand. But the short story is, in my view, the most difficult form of fiction to master. So why try? Two reasons: First, when it works, it can be one of the most powerful reading experiences there is. And second, with digital self-publishing, there's an actual market for these works again. The short story form was pretty much dead outside of a few journals. Now, in digital you can make some Starbucks money with them. That's what the *Force of Habit* and *Irish Jimmy Gallagher* stories have done for me. And when I put together a collection, I expect to make even more.

And nothing will give your writing chops a workout like a short story. Why not make them part of your career plan?

If you want to learn more, here are some great collections:

Literary

The short stories of Ernest Hemingway, Flannery O'Connor, Raymond Carver, John Cheever, Irwin Shaw

Crime

Enough Rope by Lawrence Block
The Best American Noir of the Century ed. by James Ellroy and Otto Penzler

Thriller

Twisted by Jeffrey Deaver

Paranormal

Stories from the Twilight Zone by Rod Serling

Classic Science Fiction

The Illustrated Man by Ray Bradbury
Masterpieces: The Best Science Fiction of the 20th Century ed. by Orson Scott Card

21. How to Write Non-Fiction

In an intriguing article in the New Jersey Star-Ledger (July 26, 2013) Allan Hoffman writes:

> Book is the new business card.
>
> That's the gist of an idea gaining currency among business coaches, social media gurus and others concerned with the brand that is you.
>
> If you're an entrepreneur, a consultant, or maybe just someone looking for an edge in the world of work, the thinking goes, you should stop obsessing about whether to use a matte or glossy finish on your business card and publish a book instead. In fact, forget the business card — you can always connect via LinkedIn. You need a book.

Hoffman quotes investor James Altucher, who say, "My bet is close to 100 percent of the people reading this post have content in them strong enough for a book."

Non-fiction freelance writing used to be a hard road for the writer. Usually you were writing articles for a one-time fee. If, that is, you could get an editor to buy something from you.

To get an editor to buy something from you, you had to establish that you were some kind of expert in the topic. Not an easy task, since you're probably not. So you'd have to become one.

Even then, to get one writing gig you probably went through hundreds of rejections. Therefore, you'd constantly be putting items in the mail, with the self-addressed and stamped return envelope to go with them. It cost money to try to get money.

What if you wanted to write a book? You'd have to get a publisher to believe that you were, guess what, an expert. And even then, you needed a "platform." What that meant was the ability to guarantee a certain number of sales before the book ever went to press.

To write history, you had to be professor somewhere. To write about health, you had to be a doctor. To write a how-to, you had to have-done and gotten famous for it.

That's all changed, because now you can publish you non-fiction book anytime you want.

Which doesn't mean you should.

Not yet.

Not until you've subjected your book to the grinder.

The Grinder

Put your idea through the following steps, one by one. Grind it up until it is refined, pure and ready to write. Skip these steps at your peril.

1. Is this a subject you are jazzed about? If not, your writing is likely to be bland and your grasp of the subject too generalized. Only tackle ideas that really grab you.

Which is not to say you can't pick a subject and then *find* the excitement in it. You can do some research, for example, and find things that you didn't know before. You can do this with some of the perennial favorite non-fiction subjects. In no particular order, they are:

Diet
Health
Love and Relationships
Cooking
Money and Finances
Business
Leadership
Spirituality
Biography
History
Humor
Cats
Dogs
Success

2. Is there a big enough market for this idea? If your subject is Biblical Skin Diseases of the Mosaic

Era, the number of buyers for your material is likely to be fairly small.

Do some research. Go to Amazon and search for books in the subject area you are considering. Check the rankings and reviews of these books. How popular are they? Can you tap into the same market?

3. Do you have a unique approach? As you research other titles in your field, root around in the book descriptions. Read the introductions. Ask yourself what you can bring to this subject that hasn't been done to death.

4. Is there a hook that might generate publicity, either locally or nationally? If you can address a hot topic, or a matter of concern to your community, it can provide an extra level of sell.

5. Do you know any experts in the subject area? Can you find some? Do you know how to conduct a proper interview?

6. Does your subject have series possibilities? A good series can be gold.

7. Come up with a list of five to ten ideas and list them in order of your interest.

8. Do preliminary research on your top idea. Read some books and articles on the subject. Even better is to identify a couple of experts and interview them. A good, quality expert is a terrific source of valuable information for your book.

9. Write an outline. This will be the skeleton of your book. All non-fiction proposals (even if you're just proposing it to yourself) need a detailed outline of the contents. It will make you analyze your topic and see what weak areas need to be addressed. Here's how to go about it:

Begin with a mind map. Mind mapping is a time-honored way to start a storm in your brain.

Get a blank piece of paper, 8.5 x 11 minimum, and a pen. Here is a shot of a little of my own mapping for this very book:

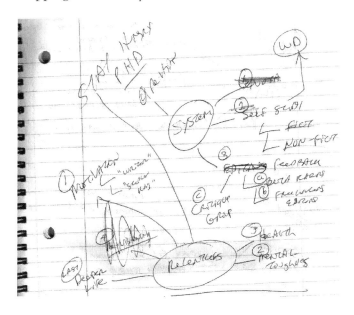

10. Organize the map with numbers and letters

You've scribbled those bubbles and lines and ideas and subjects and sub-topics. That's the fun part. Now look at what you've done and start to put some sort of order to it. This isn't as hard as it might seem. You're looking for a logical sequence, a flow.

Let's say you choose a topic to be #1. Put a 1 with a circle around it there. If that topic has led to sub-topics, letter those with a, b, c and so on.

11. Create an outline according to the numbers

This is the part that will remind you most of school. Probably the part you hated. It's much easier now, isn't it? No grade!

12. Refine and add to the outline

Let the outline cool off for a day. Come back to it and see what else you can add. Do this again if you so desire.

13. Turn your outline's main subjects into grabber chapter titles

This step is going to render your table of contents. You want your contents to communicate the "sizzle" of your book. It's a selling point. Browsers and samplers are going to judge your book's worth partly on the TOC.

One of my favorite books on old-school freelancing is *Too Lazy to Work, Too Nervous to Steal* by John Clausen. Here are some of his chapter titles:

Mamas, Don't Let Your Babies Grow Up to Be Wage Slaves

Making a Great Living as a Freelancer Isn't as Hard as You Might Think!

What's the Big Idea?

Breaking and Entering

Pitching, Schmoozing and Maintenance Lunching

Lessons Learned From a Master Teacher

The Importance of Being Flamboyant

Editors May Forgive, But They Never Forget

Another good book on this very subject of non-fiction writing has a great title: *Damn! Why Didn't I Write That?* by Marc McCutcheon. That grabs your attention. Then there's the subtitle: *How Ordinary People are Raking in $100,000 or More Writing Nonfiction Books & How You Can Too!*

What a mouthful! But does it tell you exactly the big idea? You bet it does. So do McCutcheon's chapter titles:

The Don't Skip This Introduction Introduction

Could You Have Written Any of These?

What Kind of Nonfiction Book Should You Write?

How to Know if Your Book Idea Will Fly

Do You Need an Agent?

213

14. Brainstorm on the chapters

Do some further brainstorming for each chapter.

For example, if one of my chapters is *The Best Way to Fight Hunger During the Day*, I'll start mind mapping or making lists. Ideas pop up, such as: snacks, water, exercise, read, chew gum, bay at the sun, drive somewhere, toothpicks, play music.

Some of those I'll toss out, of course. Baying at the sun was one of those things my mind generated that I wrote down (remember, no judging during mind mapping).

Now I can think about these sub-topics and organize them with numbers, just as I did with the main topics.

Most of the time these sub-topics will be headings within the chapters. Headings and lists and bullet points make the text easy to read.

Writing the Book

Once you've gone through the grinder, you are ready to write! It will go so much faster and easier now that you've done this work. Time to pour out your genius. Follow these steps:

1. Jam write your way through the outline

Jam writing is the practice of writing as much content as you can in a given writing stint. When you jam, you don't pause to edit for style or logic. You write as much as you can as each thought occurs to you. Only when you finish a session do you assess and edit and organize your writing.

See the similarity with mind mapping?

If you write out some content and find yourself hitting a wall, not knowing what to write next, put in a symbol as a marker to come back to. I use three asterisks. Later on I'll search for these and see what I need to flesh out.

But for jam writing purposes, put in the asterisks and then drop two spaces and start on a completely new thought.

Do this until you feel you've exhausted the sub-topic.

Write in a conversational style. If you can talk and make sense, you can write a non-fiction book. Don't use a ten dollar word when a buck will do. You're not writing to impress but to educate, inform and entertain.

2. Assess the jammed pages and fill in the gaps

When it's time to edit, you go through and fill in the gaps. With what? Isn't that why you stopped in the first place?

Here are a few suggestions:

• An authoritative quote that supports your point.

• Content that you gain by further research.

• An anecdote from someone you know or that you find in a news account (be sure to give the citation).

• An illustration. This is something you make up to illustrate the point. For example, you're writing your diet book. At the end of a jam-write sentence you've written: *You'll want to quit that first day.* ***

The three asterisks are the gap. For an illustration, make something up. Like this:

Imagine you're a marathon runner. You've made the declaration you're going to run in the next L.A. Marathon. But you're woefully out of shape. You decide to get in shape. You walk around the block and feel winded. Do you give up the following morning?

No way. You visualize yourself in the L.A. Marathon, get out of bed, and walk a little faster around the block — after you've put on your jogging togs, of course.

3. Know your subject and don't parrot others

It's possible to cobble together a book on a subject you are only tangentially interested in, just to make some dough.

You can cut and paste material from the internet.

You know what will happen if you do that? People will pick up that you've done that and leave you scathing reviews.

On the other hand, if a subject truly engages you then you can do a thing called research. You can study, interview experts, give yourself some experiences and make yourself a guinea pig.

In all of this keep asking yourself what your USP (Unique Selling Proposition) is going to be. If you want to write a biography of John Wayne, how are you going to be different from all the other biographies?

If you're going to write a diet book, what will you add that others haven't already said?

Then there are those who copy someone else's work and just change some of the wording around. This is called plagiarism. Plagiarizing is the lowest form of writing It's not even writing. It's theft. You can try to get away with it but sooner or later it'll bite you in the butt. When it does, you'll find yourself banned from Amazon as well as polite society.

Which doesn't mean you can't write a book on the same subject as someone else. Just make sure you are doing your own thinking and research and writing.

If, during your research, you come across an idea from another author that fits in your book, be sure to give that other author credit and a citation, so others can check out the material.

Just don't fill your book with too many clips, even with attribution. It gets annoying and will make it seem like you're just cutting and pasting.

Be a sincere scholar when it comes to the subject you've chosen. Follow the rules of a good research paper. If you don't know those rules, look them up.

Here, for example, is a clip from U.C. Berkeley's library website on the matter of avoiding plagiarism:

> Whenever you quote or base your ideas on another person's work, you must document the source you used. Even when you do not quote directly from another work, if reading that source contributed to the ideas presented

in your paper, you must give the authors proper credit.

Citations allow readers to locate and further explore the sources you consulted, show the depth and scope of your research, and give credit to authors for their ideas. Citations provide evidence for your arguments and add credibility to your work by demonstrating that you have sought out and considered a variety of resources. In written academic work, citing sources is standard practice and shows that you are responding to this person, agreeing with that person, and adding something of your own. Think of documenting your sources as providing a trail for your reader to follow to see the research you performed and discover what led you to your original contribution.

4. Communicate benefits

People read non-fiction to learn things that will benefit their lives. That can be history, how-to, exposé, narrative non-fiction, biography, recipes and so on.

Which means you have to know what the benefits of your material are, and be able to communicate them in a clear and distinct way. Which leads to:

5. Develop a personal style

Find your own voice and fit the voice to the material. When you read Dave Barry, you know what you're going to get—goofy, off-the-wall, hilarious.

When you read David McCullough, you also know what you're going to get—thorough, engaging, compelling.

Neither of these voices comes easy, by the way. Writing is work. Writing well is harder work.

Writing books that sell big is the hardest work of all. Which means:

6. Avoid fluff

Fluff is the stuff that is not helpful and takes up too much space. It is the kind of material that has the reader thinking, Get to the point already!

It is material that is barely relevant to the book's central thesis or message, yet goes on and on.

There is no meter or gauge or alarm to go off to tell you you're over-fluffing. You just have to be aware of it.

If you find yourself thinking, I can make this book a little longer if I add more words…you're probably thinking fluffy.

7. Finish what you write

You can't edit what isn't there. Words to live by.

8. Let the book sit for a week

So you can come back to it with objectivity and freshness.

9. Begin editing

As I said before, I like to print out a hard copy for this. It makes notes and marks on the page easier.

10. Learn your craft as you edit

For me, the best book on writing non-fiction is the classic by William Zinsser, *On Writing Well.* You also need a basic book on grammar (or a go-to website) so you can use the language.

Let me tell you why. Some time ago I read a column on the website of a leading sports magazine. The column was discussing fan disappointment in a professional basketball coach, because he had not gotten his team into the NBA finals. Then there was this sentence:

Coach X's criticism spawns from what his team has not accomplished.

Now, can you tell what is wrong with that horrible strangulation of the English language? I'll wait.

Okay, I'm back.

First of all, the thought that was intended was turned into its very opposite.

By using a possessive ('s) the sentence is telling us that the subject is Coach X's criticism, NOT criticism OF Coach X, which is what the whole story is about!

Then there is the phrase *spawns from* which the writer apparently thinks means the same thing as *springs from*. Only it doesn't, for spawning produces, it isn't produced.

Yes, grammar matters, or eventually no one will know what you're talking about and soon enough we'll all be grunting at each other like the Eloi from *The Time Machine*.

So learn to write.

The Cover

Sometime during your initial writing (or even before) you ought to give some thought to your cover. Get in the habit of saving covers you see online that appeal to you. Research the kinds of covers the most popular books in your subject area have.

Remember, you want a cover that will show up nicely as a thumbnail as an Amazon alsobot (the covers that appear in the "customers also bought" section of an Amazon book page).

There are "cheap" ways to design a cover. Remember, you get what you pay for and your cover is one of your most important selling points. Believe me, the extra money you spend on your cover will be more than made up in the extra sales you make.

See the steps on cover design in the Short Course on Self-Publishing chapter.

The Edit

Print out a hard copy of your draft. I prefer this to the ereader for note taking and scribbling purposes.

Read through as if you were a reader coming upon this book for the first time. As you do, keep the following in mind:

• Cut clutter

Clutter is the term for useless words that fill up a page like weeds infest a lawn. It was popularized by the great Zinsser in *On Writing Well*.

When editing, look for places where you can get rid of words that just don't need to be there.

Take the sentence I just wrote. It's puffed up with clutter. Better would be this: When editing, get rid of the words that don't need to be there.

There's no formula for getting rid of clutter. I can't say I'm as careful about it as I should be. You need to do a dedicated "clutter edit" to seek and destroy wasted words.

Here are three examples of clutter, and what you can substitute:

Prior to the invention of...
Before the invention of...

It appears there are two things to...
There are two things to...

It's a fact that during World War II....
During World War II...

You get the idea. Your writing almost always improves when you cut. Don't be afraid to be a surgeon.

• Avoid clichés like the plague

You'll find them, those hackneyed phrases that usually glaze the eyes of readers. Things like:

At the end of the day.
Nothing could be further from the truth.
If the shoe fits, wear it.

You get the idea. Cut them or freshen them up. The science fiction writer Harlan Ellison once wrote the line, *She looked like a million bucks.* Cliché. So he gave it a new gleam: *She looked like a million bucks tax free.*

A cliché won't kill you, and sometimes you can use one as shorthand. But keep their use to a minimum.

• Strive for clarity

In a non-fiction book, you need to be clear. You want the reader to take in information and understand it. You don't want to leave them scratching their heads. (Oops, that's a cliché. How about *scratching their domes...*)

• Shorten sentences

A newspaper editor once yelled at a cub reporter, "The period is the greatest tool in the English

223

language. Use it!" He was trying to train a college kid to communicate, not impress a professor.

Short sentences work. They have punch. They make the reading easier.

Try using more periods in your book.

Once you've been over your draft and cleaned it up, it's time for your ...

Beta and Proof Readers

As with fiction, beta readers are a tremendous value. But instead of reading for plot and character, they will be seeing if your non-fiction book is easy to read and useful in application.

Once you get their feedback, you do a second draft. Give it spell check.

Then hire a proofreader.

Typos still happen, even in books from the big publishing houses. Readers may alert you to a typo or two when your book is live, but as a self-publisher those will be easy to fix. Also, Amazon's Kindle site has a pretty good spotter when you upload your content.

You're done!

Upload the book or sell it to a major publisher for millions of dollars.

One of these two scenarios is more likely than the other. I'll leave it to you which step to take.

22. Add Audio-Books for More Income

According to an article in *The Wall Street Journal* (Aug. 1, 2013) there is an "explosion" in the production and consumption of audio books. Authors, especially those self-publishing, take note:

> "We're moving toward a media-agnostic consumer who doesn't think of the difference between textual and visual and auditory experience," says Don Katz, Audible's founder and CEO. "It's the story, and it is there for you in the way you want it."

Audio books have ballooned into a $1.2 billion industry, up from $480 million in retail sales in 1997. Unit sales of downloaded audio books grew by nearly 30% in 2011 compared with 2010, according to the Audio Publishers Association. Now they can be downloaded onto smartphones with the tap of a finger, often for the price of an e-book.

This development is not without its critics and concerns.

> The rapid rise of audio books has prompted some hand-wringing about how we consume literature. Print purists doubt that listening to a book while multitasking delivers the same experience as sitting down and silently reading. Scientific studies have repeatedly shown that for competent readers, there is virtually no difference between listening to a story and reading it. The format has little bearing on a reader's ability to understand and remember a text. Some scholars argue that listening to a text might even improve understanding, especially for difficult works like Shakespeare, where a narrator's interpretation of the text can help convey the meaning.

Despite the doubts, it's clear that audio is not only here to stay, it's going to grow. Which means another income stream for authors.

If you are going it alone, the path to a recorded version of your work couldn't be simpler. The ACX program at Amazon has one of the most user-friendly programs in publishing.

ACX was created by Audible, the world's leading producer of downloadable media. Audible was subsequently bought by Amazon. Works that are produced via ACX are available on Audible's site, Amazon and the iTunes store.

Set up an account at ACX.com (you will be using the same user name and password that you use for your Kindle account).

Currently, you can choose three different ways to produce an audio for ACX.

1. You audition and choose a narrator, and share the proceeds 50/50. No up-front costs to you. You choose the type of narrative voice you're looking for and upload a portion of your manuscript. ACX lists the audition for its network of narrators. When someone uploads their sample narration, you will be notified and can listen to it online.

2. You audition and negotiate with narrators to pay them for their services. This obviously means a substantial investment, but you also get to keep all of the royalties. The question is whether you think you can sell enough in audio to justify the expense.

3. You do your own reading and producing and upload to ACX. The issue here is time and professional quality. It's not easy to read well. Still, don't let being an "amateur" stop you. Stephen King's voice is not the most mellifluous and he's done a lot of his books.

If you do want to explore this angle, have a look at ACX's resources for authors thinking about narrating their work. You might want to try it first with a short book and see how you do.

Production possibilities will become ever more creative, sort of like old time radio. Max Brooks spent a year putting together a version of his novel, World War Z, with 40 different voices. "Audio books to a great extent used to be just another way of milking the cow," he says. "Now because there is such demand and the production value is so inexpensive, it opens the door for more creative storytelling."

When your audio book is available for sale, check out soundcloud.com, where you can create an audio clip of your book and post it on your website. This "free sample" is an easy way for potential buyers to test your wares.

23. Managing Your Time

I know how busy you are. And I know you are interested in making a living as a writer.

We have to reconcile those two things.

That's why I've written this chapter on how to manage your time and your life. Some of this material I've mentioned in passing. Now I want to put it all together in a systematic way.

I'm going to give you these principles in the most efficient way I can. You are free to use them, adapt them, make them work for you. All with the goal of increasing your efficiency, productivity and overall happiness.

Yes, happiness. I've discovered that the people who know what they're doing with time, which is after all our only real commodity, are the happiest people. They get the most done and are more likely to accomplish their goals.

While there are many courses out there on time management, which you could pay up to $500 or maybe even more to take, I just don't see the point. I'm going to give you everything you need to know about managing your time and your life right here (by the way, there's a great little book that is sadly out of print called *How to Get Control of Your Time and Your Life* by Alan Lakein. Pick up a used copy if you want to delve further into time management. *Time Power* by Brian Tracy is another excellent resource).

Once you start practicing these methods, you'll be amazed at your increase in efficiency. It will almost be as if you are creating an extra hour in the day, and one that is productive to boot.

But first a couple of provisos.

This is not about becoming a military-style time nut. You have to have balance in life. What I'm giving you are only tools, and it's up to you to use them wisely.

I advocate taking time to loaf. Yes, schedule lazy time. For most of my life I've worked for myself, as a lawyer, entrepreneur, and writer. I have thus always been in charge of my own schedule. Early on I read something by Jay Conrad Levinson, the man who wrote the guerrilla series of books. In *The Way of the Guerrilla: Achieving Success and Balance as an Entrepreneur in the 21st Century*, Levinson extolled the value of taking Friday afternoons off. A simple suggestion, but one that I found I absolutely looked forward to. It made me work all the harder during the week just so I could loaf on Friday afternoon.

That's just an example of the flexibility you'll have when you know how to manage time.

First, I'm going to give you the 20 Power Tools for managing time. These will transform your life. Guaranteed.

Then I'll conclude with sections on how to handle problems and stress.

Let's manage.

The 20 Power Tools

1. Plan your weeks

The absolute number one rule of time management is you have to plan in advance. And the best way to plan is by the week.

I like to take some time on Sunday and look at the week ahead on the calendar. The first thing I do is mark every block of time where I have an obligation. These things could be work related, family related, whatever.

Once those are marked on the calendar, I'm free to start filling up the rest of the slots with prioritized tasks (see #2, below). This takes maybe five minutes to do, because I know already the tasks I need to perform.

2. Prioritize your tasks

Make a list of all the things you want and have to do, a master list of as many things you can think of.

You're going to put these tasks into three different categories.

The first category is those tasks that you *must* do. You absolutely have to complete these things in order to accomplish your goals and do your work well.

Put an A next to each item in this category.

Next, look for those important matters that you would *like* to get to if you can. Mark those items with a B.

Finally, select the items on your list that can wait or are optional. Those you mark with the letter C.

Now go through each letter group and prioritize those tasks. For example, your most important A task you will designate as A-1. Your next most important A task is A-2.

Do the same with the Bs and Cs.

Finally, put a time estimate next to each task. For example, if your A-1 task is to complete a report that's due on Friday, and you know it's going to take you about two hours, put a 2 next to it. I put my letters at the beginning and my time estimates at the end, like this:

A-1 Finish the report on dental floss distribution. 2

A-2 Start research on new sources of dental floss 1.5

All this doesn't take long to do once you're used to it, and the benefits are immediate. You won't have to guess what to schedule for your week, or what task to tackle next during the day. You'll have the plan all set out for you.

Be somewhat flexible. If some urgent task pops up, find the right place for it on your list and adjust the other items.

Make a new list every week, eliminating those tasks that no longer apply and adding whatever new ones you need.

3. Take advantage of your best hour of the day

Everybody has one hour where they feel the most creative, energetic, sharp and good looking. For many people that comes in the morning. For me it's about half an hour into my day, after I've started on that first cup of coffee. I like to wake up early, when it's still dark, and start the coffee going for my wife who is still snoozing quietly away. I then take my cup and go to the computer.

Find your own favorite hour. It might be at night when the kids are finally asleep. Or maybe it's when you're at Starbucks at noon and the espresso starts to kick in.

Whatever it is, determine to take full advantage of that hour. Put your head down and work. Do not check your phone or your e-mail. Do not go on Twitter or Facebook. Do not pass Go. Do not collect $200.

You can probably get three times more done in this one hour than you will at any other hour during your day.

4. Do one thing at a time

Forget multi-tasking when you work. Put full concentration on the task at hand.

What you're trying to get to is a sense of *Flow,* as described by psychologist Mihaly Csíkszentmihályi in his book of the same name. This is a state of deep, immersive attention. When it happens, you are at your best mentally and creatively. You know this in part because time seems to speed up.

Another term for this state is being in "the zone." You get it from doing just one thing at a time.

5. Take short breaks

You can't efficiently concentrate on something indefinitely. Studies show that if you focus hard for about fifty minutes, then take a ten minute break, your efficiency will optimize.

If you are at a workplace with a Lumbergh watching you (see the movie *Office Space)* you'll need to find a way to rest your brain for a few minutes.

It's not hard to do.

Sit up straight in your chair, close your eyes, and take five long, slow breaths. As you do, count down from five. 5-4-3-2-1. Then slowly open your eyes and take one more deep breath. If you can wear headphones and listen to some soft or classical music (or ocean sounds) try that for a few minutes. Imagine you're sitting on a nice beach. Smell the suntan lotion.

Take your full lunch hour. Don't work at your desk.

"Half our life is spent trying to find something to do with the time we have rushed through life trying to save." – Will Rogers

6. Take a real rest one day a week

Use one whole day per week for creative leisure. Read. Learn a new subject. Get courses from The Teaching Company (an outstanding resource!). But also this: Use part of the day for pure loafing. That's right. We live in such a hurry-up world. It's possible to fill every second with some sort of activity. Down time is almost unheard of. We can be Tweeting or Facebooking, texting, playing Angry Birds or any of an infinite number of games. If you don't learn to shut out the noise for at least part of your week, you'll be more tired and just plain disagreeable than you otherwise might be. And we have to live with you. So loaf.

7. Use Google Reader to quickly go through relevant material

Using Google Reader enables you to pick blogs and feeds that impact your life and skim the headlines. Don't be sucked into the trap of reading everything.

If you get printed magazines or newsletters, go quickly over the contents and tear out the articles you want to read. Save those for down time, when you're waiting in line and the like. Toss the rest of the magazine in the can.

8. Set aside time for email and social media

Do not approach these tasks haphazardly. Schedule time for them or they'll suck the time out of you.

9. Learn how to power nap

I take a power nap each day during my zombie phase, which is, for me, 2 – 4 p.m. I put my feet up on my desk, or go lie down, and am out for 15 – 20 minutes. That's it. You can learn to do this. It takes a little time, but your body will soon cooperate. I estimate I get an hour and a half of more productive time in the evening if I take a power nap in the afternoon.

After your power nap, drink a big glass of water and down a few almonds or walnuts with raisins.

10. Throughout the day ask, "What's the best use of my time right now?"

Even if it's only for thirty seconds at a time, get in this habit. If you save a few minutes, those minutes accumulate.

11. Make TV your slave, not the other way around

DVR news programs so you can whip through them instead of watching them live. Consider doing the same for sports, so you can fast forward during time outs and commercials. Make a game of seeing how much TV you can do without.

"Time flies like an arrow. Fruit flies like a banana." – Groucho Marx

12. Reward yourself when you have reached a significant milestone

When I finish a manuscript I like to take a full day off and go on a literary goof. There are used bookstores in L.A. I like, so I'll start there, browse the shelves, pick up that Cornell Woolrich I've been missing, or add to my collection of 50's paperback originals. I might just go to a park or the beach, put out a chair and read. That night, I'll take my wife to one of our favorite places for dinner. You simply have to enjoy the journey or what's the point of it all?

13. Eat a light lunch so you don't get draggy in the afternoon

Salad. Tuna. Chicken. Fruit.
Drink plenty of water.

14. Learn how to skim books

This is a little harder to do in the age of the e-reader. I prefer printed non-fiction so I can quickly scan the table of contents and chapters and individual pages. The secret to skimming is to create questions you want the book to answer. That way, you're not so concerned with reading cover to cover. You can read looking only for the relevant passages. No law says you have to read every word of every book.

15. Always have something to read for "waiting" times

At the very least, have something queued up on your smart phone.

"Great moments in science: Einstein discovers that time is actually money." — Gary Larson, *The Far Side* cartoon caption

16. Master 80/20 thinking

Recall that, generally, eighty percent of your results come from twenty percent of your activities. Or the other way around, twenty percent of what you do is going to determine eighty percent of your results. If, for example, you have a list of ten items on your current To Do list, two of them are going to be the most important tasks to perform.

Identify them and do them first.

17. Delegate as much as you can

If there is any way to get someone else to perform lower level tasks for you, even if it costs you a little money, hire them. Save your own time for the most important things you have to do your own sweet self.

18. Handle each correspondence only once

Be it paper or email correspondence, deal with it immediately. If it doesn't demand a response, don't respond.

19. Learn the art of "snatching" time

You can prepare to use "off" times productively. In your car, instead of always listening to music, listen to a self-study course. When you go to the doctor or dentist, bring a project with you. When you fly somewhere, plan to use eighty percent of the flight time doing something productive, not playing games or watching movies.

For long flights I always bring something to edit, something to read, and my computer to write on.

I get a window seat so I won't have anyone piling over me to get to the bathroom.

"We are here on Earth to do good to others. What the others are here for, I don't know." – W. H. Auden

20. Find something higher to live for

Life is not about you alone. It's about relationships and giving and making the world a better place. The happiest people on earth are those who find a way to give something back. Be one of those people.

And please read the next chapter.

24. Make a Life, Not Just a Living

We've been talking about making a living as a
writer. We've covered the most important things you
have to do to increase the odds of making that
happen.

Now I want to focus more on the *living* part.
Because you can easily, so easily, fall into a trap that
drains the joy out of your life.

That trap is *obsession*.

This writing life presents us with a never-ending
cornucopia of things we can do to try to get *more*.
Even when you've reached a certain level of success,
you'll find yourself lusting after even greater rewards.

Or recognition.

You'll do things out of a restless energy that is
fueled by this choking desire for more. That, in turn,
will grow weeds around the other parts of your life,
your relationships with loved ones most of all.

You might start to lose sleep.

You'll be in this swirl of discontent that never
seems to go away.

Don't go there.

Ancient Wisdom

One of the worst developments of our time is the disregard for ancient wisdom. Universities don't emphasize it anymore. The idea that there are standards which have stood the test of time and should be passed down through the generations is considered a quaint nostrum from the past.

To quote Puck, what fools we mortals be.

The ancients knew that we are creatures of lust. Not just in the sexual arena, but in the *desire for more and the envy of others who have it.*

This is the very antithesis of happiness. As Buddha said, "Desires are never satisfied, not even by a shower of gold. He who knows that the enjoyment of passion is short-lived and that it is also the womb of pain is a wise man."

The ancients knew that even if one gains all that one desires, it still does not satisfy. Solomon wrote, "Then I looked on all the works that my hands had wrought, and on the labour that I had laboured to do: and, behold, all was vanity and vexation of spirit, and there was no profit under the sun."

In a *New York Times* opinion piece (July 18, 2014),Arthur Brooks wrote about Abd al-Rahman, a 10th century caliph in Cordobá, Spain. Like King Solomon, he had wealth and pleasures in greater abundance than any other man of his time. Yet at the end of his life he said, "I have diligently numbered the days of pure and genuine happiness which have fallen to my lot: They amount to fourteen."

So rather than making him happy, these external things brought the opposite. Brooks, in the piece, offers this as a reason:

Have you ever known an alcoholic? They generally drink to relieve craving or anxiety — in other words, to attenuate a source of unhappiness. Yet it is the drink that ultimately prolongs their suffering. The same principle was at work for Abd al-Rahman in his pursuit of fame, wealth and pleasure.

But it's not just wealth so many of us crave, it's also recognition. We want to be seen by others as a success, and we want others to acknowledge that.

This is a modern cancer because of the rise in social media. As Brooks explains:

Today, each of us can build a personal little fan base, thanks to Facebook, YouTube, Twitter and the like. We can broadcast the details of our lives to friends and strangers in an astonishingly efficient way. That's good for staying in touch with friends, but it also puts a minor form of fame-seeking within each person's reach. And several studies show that it can make us unhappy.

It makes sense. What do you post to Facebook? Pictures of yourself yelling at your kids, or having a hard time at work? No, you post smiling photos of a hiking trip with friends.

You build a fake life — or at least an incomplete one — and share it. Furthermore, you consume almost exclusively the fake lives of your social media "friends." Unless you are extraordinarily self-aware, how could it not make you feel worse to spend part of your time pretending to be happier than you are, and the other part of your time seeing how much happier others seem to be than you?

Yes, part of marketing ourselves as writers involves social media. But unless we are very aware of what we're doing and how we're doing it, the tangles of discontent will grow around our spirit.

Brooks concludes by asserting that we need to develop "a deep skepticism of our own basic desires. Of course you are driven to seek admiration, splendor and physical license. But giving in to these impulses will bring unhappiness. You have a responsibility to yourself to stay in the battle. The day you declare a truce is the day you become unhappier."

I'm not saying it's easy to get rid of these desires. If it were, we wouldn't need the teachings of religion and philosophy.

But here we are, striving and doing and setting goals. That's all good. That's all positive. But at the same time, remember what I said earlier about slaying *expectations*. Do everything in your power not to expect too much. When good things start to happen, you will enjoy them all the more.

Nourish a life outside your writing.

Family.

Friends.

Do something for somebody without expecting anything back.

Explore your spirit. Challenge yourself. Even if you end up believing exactly the same things, study and reflection on higher things will take your mind off materialism for awhile. That's healthy for *everybody*.

What I'm trying to say here is never put all your happiness eggs into the basket of your publishing enterprise. Writing and publishing are part of your life, but they're not your whole life.

25. Essential Resources

Good writers are good readers. Below is a list of some of my favorite books, in no particular order. I chose some of them for their style as much as their subject. I've not made any attempt to be complete or "correct" here. This is a highly personal list of books that have helped me become a better writer.

Some of these titles might not be to your particular taste. But I encourage you to read outside your normal comfort zone. Doing that will stretch and strengthen you, and give your writer's brain more nourishment.

NON-FICTION:

The Last Lion: A Biography of Winston Churchill, William Manchester (3 volumes)
The Executioner's Song, Norman Mailer
In Cold Blood, Truman Capote
A Civil Action, Jonathan Harr
Truman, David McCullough
Bradbury Speaks, Ray Bradbury

All Over But the Shoutin', Rick Bragg
The Electric Kool-Aid Acid Test, Tom Wolfe
The Norton Book of Personal Essays, Joseph Epstein, ed.
The Writer Who Stayed, William Zinsser

FICTION:

Farewell, My Lovely, Raymond Chandler
The Maltese Falcon, Dashiell Hammett
Rebecca, Daphne DuMaurier
My Name is Aram, William Saroyan
To Kill a Mockingbird, Harper Lee
The Hunger Games, Suzanne Collins
The Bonfire of the Vanities, Tom Wolfe
On the Road, Jack Kerouac
Different Seasons, Stephen King
Short Stories, Ernest Hemingway
Fahrenheit 451, Ray Bradbury
Lost Light, Michael Connelly
Tell No One, Harlan Coben

HOW TO WRITE:

Non-Fiction

On Writing Well, William Zinsser
The Elements of Style, Strunk & White
How Not to Write, Terrence Denman
How to Write a Book Proposal, Michael Larsen
Writing in Overdrive: Write Faster, Write Freely, Write Brilliantly, Jim Denney

MARKETING:

BUSINESS AND COPYWRITING:

CREATIVITY:

The 3 A.M. Epiphany, Brian Kiteley
Hatch!: Brainstorming Secrets of a Theme Park Designer,
C. McNair Wilson
*A Whack on the Side of the Head: How You Can Be
More Creative,* Roger von Oech

26. A Final Word

You are a writer.

You will write and not grow weary. You will type and not faint.

You are a writer.

Inside you there are universes. You contain multitudes.

Tap them.

Zap them.

And create some more.

You are a writer, and no one can tell you that you are not. If someone dares to say you don't have what it takes, quietly cross them off your worth-listening-to list. You don't have time for that bunk. Your time is better spent writing some more.

You're a writer, so you honor the craft. Don't look at success like the granite-jawed star quarterback looks at the head cheerleader ("I deserve her just because I exist!"). Success is something you earn by working hard and intelligently.

You are a writer, which means you write even if you get discouraged. Because there's always the next book and you won't stop writing because it's what you love.

There is more opportunity than ever to get paid for your work. It's the greatest time on earth to be a writer.

And that's what you are.

Carpe Typem!
Seize the Keyboard!

Thanks for reading *How to Make a Living as a Writer*. It's my great pleasure to build up writers as they pursue their dreams. If you would like to be on my email list, and be among the first to know about my new books and deals, please take a moment to sign up on my website: www.jamesscottbell.com.

Most of all, keep writing.

Printed in Great Britain
by Amazon.co.uk, Ltd.,
Marston Gate.